101 Ways to Make Yourself Indispensable at Work

Carol A. Silvis, M.Ed.

Course Technology PTR

A part of Cengage Learning

COURSE TECHNOLOGY
CENGAGE Learning‑

Australia, Brazil, Japan, Korea, Mexico, Singapore, Spain, United Kingdom, United States

COURSE TECHNOLOGY
CENGAGE Learning™

101 Ways to Make Yourself Indispensable at Work
Carol A. Silvis, M. Ed.

Publisher and General Manager, Course Technology PTR:
Stacy L. Hiquet

Associate Director of Marketing:
Sarah Panella

Manager of Editorial Services:
Heather Talbot

Marketing Manager:
Mark Hughes

Acquisitions Editor:
Mitzi Koontz

Project Editor:
Sandy Doell

Editorial Services Coordinator:
Jen Blaney

Copy Editor:
Heather Kaufman Urschel

Interior Layout Tech:
Bill Hartman

Cover Designer:
Mike Tanamachi

Indexer:
BIM Indexing & Proofing Services

Proofreader:
Sandi Wilson

Course Technology, a part of Cengage Learning
20 Channel Center Street
Boston, MA 02210
USA

For product information and technology assistance, contact us at **Cengage Learning Customer & Sales Support, 1-800-354-9706**

For permission to use material from this text or product, submit all requests online at **cengage.com/permissions**. Further permissions questions can be e-mailed to **permissionrequest@cengage.com**.

All trademarks are the property of their respective owners.

Library of Congress Control Number: 2009927801

ISBN-13: 978-1-4354-5432-3

ISBN-10: 1-4354-5432-4

Cengage Learning is a leading provider of customized learning solutions with office locations around the globe, including Singapore, the United Kingdom, Australia, Mexico, Brazil, and Japan. Locate your local office at: **international.cengage.com/region**.

Cengage Learning products are represented in Canada by Nelson Education, Ltd.

For your lifelong learning solutions, visit **courseptr.com**.

Visit our corporate Web site at **cengage.com**.

Printed in Canada
1 2 3 4 5 6 7 11 10 09

This book is dedicated to the memory of my dad,
Edward M. Baer, whose creativity for going
beyond the ordinary inspired me.

ACKNOWLEDGMENTS

A special thanks to Mitzi Koontz, Acquisitions Editor, for her vision and support with this project; to Sandy Doell, Project Editor, for her expertise and assistance; and to Heather Urschel, Copy Editor, for her insight and guidance. It was a pleasure working with such a fine team of professionals. Thanks also to the many others who had a hand in producing this book. Thank you, Martine Edwards, for pointing me in the right direction in my writing career.

I would like to acknowledge my supportive family—Ryan, Niki, and Mikaila—for their encouragement and my parents, Rosella and Harold Miller.

Thanks to Newport Business Institute for the encouragement and to the Tiani family at Watson's for supporting my need to write.

ABOUT THE AUTHOR

Carol Silvis is the author of the college textbooks *100% Externship Success* (Cengage Learning 2009) and *General Office Procedures* (Cengage Learning 2001) and a dozen creative non-fiction stories and inspirational pieces published in national magazines.

For over two decades, Carol Silvis has trained adults in how to get a job, keep and enjoy it, and get ahead. She has a master's degree in Adult Education and is an associate director and department chair at Newport Business Institute. In addition, she gives talks and workshops to businesses and organizations on a wide range of business topics.

Ms. Silvis has appeared on Cornerstone TV and has been interviewed for radio and newspapers. She is vice president of Pennwriters, Inc., received the 2008 Meritorious Service Award, and was the 2005 and 2007 Conference Coordinator.

Visit her website www.carolsilvis.com and blog www.carolsilvis.blogspot.com.

Contents

INTRODUCTION

101 Ways to Make Yourself Indispensable at Work comprises 101 of what I have come to know are the best ways to build a successful career. Employers are looking for work savvy professionals who have the attitude, determination, and motivation to meet their needs, and if you apply each of these 101 ways to your own career, you will find yourself a valued, *indispensable*, employee.

In the first four chapters of this book, you will learn how to focus on developing positive work habits that increase proficiency and personal ethical standards. Learn how to begin to make your attitude at work more positive, get excited about your job, get along well with your peers, and more.

Chapter 5, "Skills and Education," presents suggestions for becoming an expert in your field and industry.

Chapter 6, "Foster People Skills," is devoted to the skills you'll need to get along better with everyone, from customers to co-workers to bosses. Here you will also learn about nonverbal ways to foster positive relationships in the workplace.

Chapter 7, "Expand Your Leadership Skills," and Chapter 8, "Strategies for Success," provide over two dozen ways to expand leadership skills and employ advancement strategies.

In Chapter 9, "Have a Plan," you will learn tips for creating your own personal plan for success.

Throughout the book, you will find exercises and self-evaluation forms that you can use to promote critical thinking, stimulate creativity, and pinpoint areas where improvement will enhance your career success.

101 Ways to Make Yourself Indispensable at Work

1. Gain a competitive edge.
2. Plan for advancement.
3. Make it happen.
4. Develop a positive attitude.
5. Take responsibility.
6. Be self-reliant.
7. Generate ideas.
8. Follow the rules.
9. Show enthusiasm.
10. Be dependable.
11. Take the initiative.
12. Show up and be punctual.
13. Be friendly and sincere.
14. Be honest.
15. Admit mistakes.
16. Be tactful.
17. Be confident.
18. Keep confidences.
19. Be realistic.
20. Keep your personal business out of the office.

21. Never discuss salary with coworkers.
22. Use good hygiene and grooming habits.
23. Learn about your boss.
24. Know your company's products and services.
25. Help your boss meet her goals.
26. Anticipate your boss's needs and make yourself invaluable.
27. Work the hours required.
28. Pull your own weight.
29. Ask for help when you need it.
30. Don't be afraid to admit you do not have all the answers.
31. Don't bad-mouth the boss, customers, and coworkers.
32. Follow the company mission statement.
33. Follow directions.
34. Don't gossip or spread rumors.
35. Give a good day's work.
36. Be flexible.
37. Be efficient.
38. Get organized.
39. Manage your time.
40. Do not abuse office equipment or take office supplies.
41. Avoid using office phones for personal business.
42. Avoid wasting company time on personal business.
43. Avoid wasting company time on the Internet.
44. Do not complain.
45. Do not waste time on idle chat.
46. Write it down.
47. Produce error-free work.
48. Consolidate tasks.
49. Manage stress.
50. Keep up to date.

81. Be a leader, not a follower.
82. Share information.
83. Remain in control of your emotions.
84. Never embarrass yourself or others at social functions.
85. Write for a company newsletter or start one.
86. Get the company involved in volunteerism.
87. Visualize success.
88. Learn how to advance within the company.
89. Be a representative for excellence.
90. Become an expert at your job.
91. Keep a record of your accomplishments.
92. Find a mentor.
93. Write a training manual.
94. Dress the part.
95. Network.
96. Maintain balance.
97. Look for ways to improve your job.
98. Follow through.
99. Set personal goals.
100. Evaluate goals.
101. Be aware of office politics.

CHAPTER 1

SURPASS THE COMPETITION

I n this book, you will find the 101 most important things you need to know not only to keep your job but also to get promotions and raises. Your challenge is to use the 101 strategies to build a solid professional reputation that will move your career in a positive direction. Make a commitment to take advantage of opportunities for self-improvement that will establish you as an indispensable employee.

Your level of commitment will have a direct result on your level of success. Adhering to these 101 strategies will make you a more promotable employee.

Throughout this book you will find checklists and questions to use in evaluating the skills and attitudes you need to improve and incorporate in your success plan. By focusing and following through, you can gain the competencies needed to ensure your maximum efficiency.

1: Gain a Competitive Edge

In today's economy, you need a competitive edge to keep your job and garner a promotion. To gain that edge, you need to excel at your job by setting high personal standards and working hard to attain them.

If you do not like the results you are getting from your job (i.e., no raise or promotion), consider your output. Do you stand out among company employees in a positive way? Do you perform your job better than your coworkers do theirs? You put forth the effort required to get the best results. Being equal will not gain you the recognition you need to get ahead. Do you need to make any changes in your behavior, work habits, and productivity to become an outstanding employee?

Look beyond yourself. What does your current position actually have to offer? Is it a rung leading up the corporate ladder? Is it enough for you to fulfill your ambitions?

TIP | Find ways to do your job better than your coworkers do theirs.

2: Plan for Advancement

When you feel you have not advanced as quickly as you think you should, try to determine where your career is stalled and why. Ask yourself these questions and answer honestly:

- Does my employer promote from within?
- Is there a suitable position for me to advance to?
- Do I have the education/skills I need to advance?
- Am I ready and prepared for a promotion/advancement?
- Do I continually look for ways to increase my value to the company?
- Do I contribute significantly to the company?
- Do I go above and beyond what is asked of me in my current position?
- Do I do my job well?
- Have my performance reviews been above average/superior?
- Are my work habits above average/superior?
- Do I meet my commitments on a consistent basis and in a timely manner?
- Do I take an active interest in my company?
- Do I keep up with industry trends?
- How well do I get along with my supervisor?
- How well do I get along with my coworkers?
- How well do I get along with customers/clients?
- Is my behavior results-oriented?
- Do I exhibit a professional demeanor at all times?

It is sometimes difficult to be personally objective when it comes to determining our worth to our employer. If after answering these questions, you feel you should have been promoted, it may be beneficial to get another opinion from someone who will be objective. One such person is your direct supervisor.

Arrange a time to sit down with your supervisor to discuss your performance and goals, and also the potential options for advancement that are available to you. Ask the supervisor what you have to accomplish to get a promotion, raise, or other distinction you are hoping to attain. Ask for specifics. Be open to a candid discussion and do not get defensive when suggestions or criticisms are offered. Remember, this is an opportunity to find out if you are performing up to your supervisor's expectations. It is also a chance to discover how to get promoted within the company and what your chances are of being promoted.

Plan for your advancement within the company by making significant contributions.

Demonstrate your willingness to learn what needs to be done, and make sure you do it accurately and effectively. Ask your supervisor for performance feedback. Such information is critical to gaining promotions. Periodically discuss your progress with the supervisor.

Other people who can evaluate your skills include coworkers and human resource personnel. The goal is to arrive at an honest understanding of your current knowledge and skills and ascertain what you still need to acquire to perform at optimum level.

You need to take an honest look at your skills and abilities to determine whether they are adequate or if you need to improve them or learn new ones. Also consider your strengths and weaknesses; find ways to eliminate weaknesses or turn them into strengths. Focus on positive work performance.

If you have been passed over for a promotion or raise, find out why. You may be thinking you lost out on a promotion or you deserve to advance, but do you really have a desire to get ahead? If you have not received a promotion and you want one, the question becomes

"What are you willing to do different to attain a promotion?" Brainstorm ideas with your boss or a trusted friend. Tailor a success plan to your specific needs to help you meet your professional goals. Then get started by concentrating on the outcome you desire. Is there something you can do right now to jump-start your career (i.e., take a class, increase your productivity, work on improving your performance reviews, etc.)?

Become a promotable person—one who uses logic and critical thinking to reach innovative decisions and is creative, motivated, and prepared to lead others. Make a positive impression on your supervisor and coworkers.

TIP   Go above and beyond what is required of you.

As you read through the chapters in this book, you will discover ways in which to enhance your professional traits and make yourself valuable in your current position and likely to be promoted in the future. Keep your standards high. Your reputation is on the line.

3: Make It Happen

One way to gain a competitive edge is to search for high-level tasks or a challenging project that will have a significant impact in the company. Keep in mind that it must be a project you can do with a high degree of success. After you find the right project, go to your supervisor and propose that you take it over or handle it. Be the first one to jump in and offer to do tasks that others do not want to do, but make sure you are qualified to do the tasks. A good way to learn new skills is to help someone who is more experienced so that you can learn how to do similar projects when the opportunity arises.

If possible, find something you can contribute that aligns with your strengths. In that way, you will have an advantage. Make sure that what you attempt to accomplish is something that clearly benefits your supervisor or the company so that it has the maximum impact.

TIP   Seek out challenging projects and tasks that will have an impact on the company.

Taking on challenging assignments is a good way to get your supervisor's attention. Looking for ways to make a significant contribution conveys that you are hard working and career-minded.

4: Develop a Positive Attitude

You have probably heard the expression "attitude is everything"; in the workplace, it takes on a special meaning. Your attitude can make or break your career; it affects how well you perform and has a direct influence on how people perceive you and how they react to you. A positive work attitude encompasses everything from displaying desirable character traits to getting along with others, accepting additional responsibility, and doing the best work possible.

A positive attitude is not merely a happy-go-lucky, smiling persona. It is an accumulation of optimistic and constructive personal traits that are displayed in a willing, consistent manner. It shows from the inside out.

So how does one go about creating the type of attitude that employers look for when hiring and promoting employees? Sometimes all it takes is a shift in thinking brought about by changing our internal dialog. Much of our negativity comes from pessimistic, unconstructive self-talk churning through our minds from morning to night. Reversing that self-talk by replacing it with upbeat, constructive language will bolster your self-esteem and ultimately your attitude.

Make a conscious effort to listen to yourself when you speak and to eliminate negative words from your vocabulary by exchanging them for more positive ones. It is likened to looking at a glass as half full rather than half empty.

Obstacles and disappointments are bound to occur throughout your career. When they do, make up your mind to seek solutions, to discover what you can do versus what you cannot do. A "cannot" attitude will invariably bring you down, whereas a "can do" attitude gives you hope.

Being aware of the attitude you project is a constant process. Some days may be frustrating or even boring as you perform the same tasks over and over. When you notice yourself becoming disapproving and cranky or unmotivated and bored, think pleasant thoughts or find some other way to cheer yourself. For instance, take a break, talk things over with someone you trust, repeat positive phrases, create and use self-motivation strategies, or let go of things you cannot control.

TIP   Evaluate the attitude you project and work on making it more positive.

Maintaining a positive attitude takes dedicated practice because you are creating a positive habit where a negative one exists. Consider these tips to build a better attitude:

- Assess your attitude—be honest with yourself.
- Continuously remind yourself to seek a constructive outcome to every situation and to do it with a positive outlook.
- Feed your mind with inspirational, motivational material.
- Turn your work into a challenge.
- Look for ways to motivate yourself.
- Take time to enjoy life and the people you love.
- Be grateful.
- Be flexible.
- Watch out for signs of depression, boredom, health problems, too little sleep, and stress, which all contribute to a decline in attitude.
- Avoid negative people.
- Keep yourself fit and healthy.
- Seek out other positive, motivated people as mentors.

5: Take Responsibility

Take personal responsibility for your actions, words, ethics, and character traits. You control your life. If you are not getting the results you want at work, readjust your thinking and actions and try something else. Admit that you always affect the outcomes in your life.

You will be held accountable for the following:

- Performance
- Behavior

- Words
- Work relationships
- Ideas
- Ideals
- Personal traits
- Skills and abilities
- Knowledge
- Attitude
- Errors and misjudgments
- Limitations and shortcomings
- Attendance and punctuality
- Decisions
- Failure to respond
- Failure to report errors, improper actions, etc.

 TIP Take personal responsibility for all your actions and words.

How often do you consciously take personal responsibility for your thoughts, words, and deeds? Answer the following questions to assess your own accountability.

Assess Your Accountability

1. Would you be dishonest if it meant saving your job?
2. How do you handle yourself when you make a mistake?
3. How would you deal with a coworker who steals your idea and claims it as his own?
4. What would you do if your boss thought your coworker's idea was your idea?
5. Do you clean up your messes in the employees' lounge?
6. Do you follow proper procedures when operating company equipment?
7. What would you do if a coworker violates safety policies?
8. Do you follow company rules and policies?

9. Do you meet deadlines?
10. Are you fair and honest in your dealings with others?
11. If you are wrong, do you admit it?
12. If you have wronged others, do you make amends?
13. Are you reliable?
14. Do you do your fair share?
15. Do you make a positive contribution to your workplace every day?
16. Do you display ethical behavior at all times?
17. Do you control your emotions?
18. Are you sincere?
19. Do you accept responsibility for and stand behind your decisions?
20. Do you get the job done when you say you will?
21. Is your language unbiased, tactful, professional, and kind?
22. Do you refrain from stealing company supplies and using company equipment for personal use?
23. Do you spend your time at work on company business?
24. Do you avoid personal calls and Internet surfing on company time?
25. Are you an asset to the company?
26. Do you accept responsibility for your actions?
27. Do you update required certifications?

 TIP Hold yourself to the highest ethical standards.

When you accept personal responsibility, you hold yourself accountable in all areas of your personal and professional life. You are honest with everyone all the time and behave in a professional manner. You admit mistakes, follow proper procedures and rules, and meet your commitments on deadline.

Look over your answers to determine your level of accountability. If you do not currently hold yourself to high standards of integrity, work to improve. If you have been disregarding policies and procedures, miss deadlines, or are unfair or emotional, begin to follow the rules and manage your time and behavior. By holding yourself accountable, you will become a valued employee.

In challenging economic times, those who refuse to accept personal and professional responsibility for their actions become liabilities to their companies. As liabilities, they set themselves up for layoffs and firings.

6: Be Self-Reliant

Employees who are self-reliant free up the boss so she can tend to other issues. After you are trained and you know what your duties are and how to complete them, do the work with minimal supervision. Refrain from running to the supervisor with every little question. Learn to think through problems and work on your own; trust your own judgment and skills.

Plan your work, prioritize, set and meet deadlines, and follow-up when necessary. Approach your supervisor only after you have exhausted other means of arriving at solutions. Having the ability to work independently sets you up for promotions by demonstrating your self-reliance and confidence.

Make sure, though, to keep your boss informed about the status of your tasks and projects—not every detail, but keep her in the loop with regard to important projects, decisions, and accomplishments.

Often the supervisory structure has mechanisms in place for providing updates and the status of projects. These can take the form of weekly status meetings, daily/weekly emails, etc. It is crucial to provide a quick, professional response to these communications. Be sure your response conveys the proper message before hitting Send as you will not be able to take it back.

The ability to work well independently inspires trust in you as an employee. Trusted employees are valued and often rewarded.

TIP Do your work with minimal supervision.

7: Generate Ideas

You can earn credibility and make a positive contribution to your company by generating viable ideas. Gain a reputation around the company of being an idea person—the one people come to when they need a better, faster, easier, or cheaper way of doing things. Resist the urge to sit back and play it safe by letting others supply the ideas. Speak up if you think your idea will save time and money or if it will make for more proficient performance.

Take stock of your own duties. Is there a more efficient way to do a task? Can you revise routine forms? Is there a way to streamline procedures? Focus on improvement.

Before incorporating changes on your own, it is wise to double-check with higher-ups. There may be specific reasons why certain procedures must be followed.

Listen to the suggestions made in brainstorming sessions to see if you can build on someone else's idea. Share ideas and information with your team members. Cooperate with them and support them. Learning new things from coworkers will broaden your knowledge base. Get as much information as possible; the better you understand policies and procedures, the easier it is to strategize.

Be creative and constructive so as to make a true contribution. When you come up with a new idea, give an example of how to implement it and why it should be considered.

TIP Be known as an "idea person."

If your idea is rejected, do not be discouraged. Find out why it was not feasible. Sometimes there may be a perception problem; sometimes there are underlying reasons why it will not work.

Continue to contribute ideas for the future. When you continue to see possibilities where there are barriers, it expands your creative mind.

To energize your creativity and continue generating ideas, increase your knowledge. Read, attend seminars and trade shows, become actively involved in brainstorming sessions, and continually challenge yourself. Focus on new and better ways of doing things.

8: Follow the Rules

Rules, regulations, guidelines, policies: these are put into place to establish a consistent structure that assures the smooth operation of the company and provides uniformity. Employees are responsible for knowing company policies and procedures, especially those spelled out in the employee handbook. They must willingly abide by these policies and ensure they meet the directives of the company. Why have rules at all if they are not properly enforced?

When an employee or group of employees abuse or disregard company policies, it sends the wrong message to supervisors, coworkers, and customers. It causes chaos, negativity, loss of productivity, low morale, and worse.

 Follow company guidelines and policies.

Employees who follow proper protocol look at the so-called rule breakers and wonder why they continue to get away with infractions. They question the special treatment the rule breakers receive when their negative behavior continues without repercussions. This disgruntles the rule followers, who begin to think observing the rules has no merit. If a few can get away with disregarding policies, why can't everyone? It causes an "If you can ignore the rules, so can I" attitude. Soon the entire office force is ignoring policies, causing upheaval and forcing the boss to take a stand.

Company policies and regulations are put in place to keep things running efficiently across the entire company, from the production department to sales and marketing, etc. When employees routinely violate policies, it creates low morale and finger pointing. Even one employee who ignores the rules can create an unpleasant situation or problem.

It is amazing how otherwise rational and responsible adults will act as if the company policies apply to everyone but them. When they break a rule, they are shocked to be reprimanded or put on notice for the infraction(s). For instance, a company may have a dress code that prohibits wearing jeans of any kind. Along comes Bob dressed in black jeans and a dress shirt. When confronted, Bob defends his wearing of black jeans, stating that they "look" like business wear. He may even go so far as to say he looks better in the jeans than some people do in their casual business slacks. Justifying his actions, Bob totally misses the point that he broke the dress code. All types of jeans are banned from the office—period.

Company rules and policies are meant for everyone—no exceptions. If you hope to continue working for a company and want to advance there, strict adherence to company policies is a must.

Rules and procedures are in effect for a reason. If you feel they do not make sense or they have little value, direct your questions to the supervisor. Some procedures may be mandated by OSHA (Occupational Safety and Health Administration) or state/local laws to comply with safety issues. Some rules may be required to keep the company running efficiently and prevent a chaotic environment.

Understanding your company's rules and procedures could provide insight into its inner workings and structure. Knowing the whys of procedures can help you understand what you need to do to keep your job and to advance in your career.

Summary

In today's tough, competitive job market, edge out the competition by building a solid professional reputation as an expert and an achiever. To advance in your career and receive recognition, perfect your skills, learn new ones, and demonstrate your value to the company through outstanding contributions.

Take on projects that have a significant impact and complete them successfully to make positive things happen in your career. Hold yourself accountable to completing duties proficiently and on time, to making viable decisions, to interacting appropriately with others, and to dealing with customers. Admit to missed deadlines and mistakes and accept responsibility for correcting the problems.

CHAPTER 2

MAKE A GOOD IMPRESSION

Your career opportunities will increase if you make a positive impression on the people for whom and with whom you work. Employers often lament their employees' lack of soft skills, such as displaying positive personal characteristics and having a work ethic essential to ensuring business success. By exhibiting dynamite personal traits and a solid work ethic, you will project a career-strengthening professional image.

In this chapter you will find a dozen personal characteristics sought by employers. Incorporating these traits into your daily life at work will help you develop and maintain the right attitude and attain career success.

9: Show Enthusiasm

Have you ever seen the expression of a hockey player who was fighting for and then scored the game winning goal? Now that is enthusiasm. Too bad we all cannot be as enthusiastic about our jobs. Or can we? What happens to the excited new hire who shows up to work the first day ready to tackle the workplace with gusto? Where does that eagerness go after a few months or years? How does she get it back? Let the boss declare an impromptu vacation day for everyone, and you will see the enthusiasm level skyrocket for that new hire and every other employee. It is important to realize that enthusiasm is something over which we have some personal control. We can decide to be enthusiastic simply by making up our minds and doing it.

We have all been helped by the waitress or bellhop or grocery bagger or salesclerk who provided service with a smile, a helpful attitude, and a zip in his step. And we have also seen those with an "I'd rather hide than help you" attitude and a lackluster personality. Why do some people in the same positions in the same or similar companies approach their jobs and lives so differently? Enthusiasm plays a big role. Enthusiastic people are more pleasant, energetic, motivated, and accomplish more in less time.

Think about it. Who wants to spend time with a dull, dreary coworker or a stone-faced supervisor? Not many of us. Listless, uninteresting people have a way of dragging everyone else in their workplace down. Learn from them what not to do. Show a zest for life and a love for your job through your actions and personality. Be a coworker others want to work with and bosses want to promote.

A note of caution: Be sure your enthusiasm is not just in your own mind but is being projected to others. For example, some job applicants interview for positions they would love to have and believe they made a positive impression during the interview process. However, they were subsequently rejected by interviewers who felt the applicants lacked enthusiasm. How is it that these interviewees believed they conveyed their interest in the job, but the interviewers detected a lack of interest? It happens more often than you might think.

It is a good idea to practice making a presentation or interviewing with a trusted friend who will give you an honest assessment of the level of enthusiasm you project during these activities. A friend could even advise you of the overall impression your attitude creates on a daily basis. During performance reviews with your boss, ask for an attitude evaluation. You might also consider finding a coach or mentor to give you necessary feedback and help you discover ways to bolster your enthusiasm.

Consider people you know or have read about who are passionate about what they do—successful businessmen and women, athletes, parents raising their children. What are these people doing that sets them apart? How do they project enthusiasm? What makes it apparent that they enjoy what they do?

Truly enthusiastic people radiate a certain passion in everything they do and say. They embrace their work and lives with open minds, hearts, and arms, and encourage others to be excited about what they do and how they do it. Enthusiastic people do not let their passion and energy fade. They rejuvenate themselves and actively look for ways to make their work and personal lives more interesting.

While genuine enthusiasm can make a huge positive difference in one's behavior, unfortunately, so can apathy. Oftentimes waning enthusiasm stems from boredom or depression. Use your creativity to turn a tedious, routine task into a challenge that interests and engages you. Do not let complacency steal your enthusiasm.

Develop your own passion and demonstrate it through a winning smile and facial expressions that mirror your excitement. Use enthusiastic voice inflections when speaking, and choose words that demonstrate a positive outlook.

Enthusiasm increases energy, which in turn boosts productivity. It inspires people and creates optimism. Enthusiastic people do not keep their enthusiasm to themselves; they share it with others. When something good happens to someone else, enthusiastic people cheer them on and celebrate with them.

Here are some good ways to develop your enthusiasm:

- Monitor your internal dialog and keep it positive.
- Add passion to your life.
- Find a job you love or a way to love your job.
- Spend some time having fun.
- Ask friends and coworkers if your passion is evident. If it is not, ask them for guidance.
- Wear your enthusiasm in your smile.
- Be enthusiastic about other people's successes.

 TIP   Let your enthusiasm show; be positive.

10: Be Dependable

Let your boss down once, and it is a strike against you. Repeatedly let her down, and your career will suffer.

Don't leave a string of unfinished tasks, broken promises, and unacceptable work. Build a reputation as someone who is unfailingly dependable—someone who can be counted on to keep his word and do the job right.

If you say you will do a task, do it. Follow through to completion when you take on a project or challenge. If you have a deadline to meet, meet it. If you make promises, keep them.

When you are not sure you can deliver on a task or a promise, do not commit to it. Always make sure you understand what is expected of you so that you know whether you can deliver the expected results on time. If you discover that you can't succeed on your own, ask someone for help or guidance so that you can deliver as promised.

Be someone supervisors can approach with an important, demanding task by efficiently completing your basic duties every day. Put your best effort into each and every job you do.

When you finish a job, follow up to ensure it was completed satisfactorily. If it wasn't, determine what you need to do to address the problems and then fix them. You may not always feel like finishing a project or following up on it, but doing so will show you are dependable and committed to success.

Answer the following questions to discover how dependable you are. Of course, the most dependable people will answer each question with *always* (and the least dependable will answer with *never*).

	Always	*Sometimes*	*Never*
Do you fully commit when you say you will do something?	____	____	____
Do you make the necessary time to work on your commitments?	____	____	____
Do you start right in on projects with little or no procrastination?	____	____	____
Do you finish what you start?	____	____	____

	Always	Sometimes	Never
Do you follow through and follow up after you have made a commitment?	_____	_____	_____
Do your friends consider you to be dependable?	_____	_____	_____
Do you keep your word when you give it?	_____	_____	_____

TIP Show up every day.

11: Take the Initiative

When you arrive at work, don't wait to get started on the day's tasks. If you know what is required of you, begin without being told. Self-starters require far less supervision, and supervisors appreciate employees who complete tasks accurately with little or no supervision (and they remember them when it is time for salary reviews and promotions).

Accomplish more than just the minimum that is expected of you. Putting forth that "little extra" effort takes you from being a mediocre employee to a valuable one, and consistently doing more than required—and doing it well—raises your visibility with management.

Seek out opportunities to prove your worth to the company. Do not be afraid to ask for additional responsibilities. Many people would rather sit back and let someone else do the work, especially when it comes to unpleasant assignments. Break out of that habit if it applies to you.

Fear often prevents people from trying something new because they do not want to look foolish or do a poor job. Overcome that fear by focusing on how to do the job well, and truly believe in yourself and your skills.

If necessary, work on building your self-esteem, skills, and knowledge so that you have the ability and mindset to do the work. Be willing to learn new things and accept the responsibility that goes with that knowledge. Develop a sense of purpose in your mind and build a connection between it and your job.

Look for ways to improve existing procedures and practices, but be aware of any boundaries that exist. Do not overstep your authority, and make sure that you always share your ideas with your boss first before you implement any changes. Ask yourself: Can I do it? Will I do it? Should I do it?

 Be a self-starter; take the initiative.

12: Show Up and Be Punctual

When employees fail to report to work or are consistently late, business suffers, coworkers are over burdened, work doesn't get completed, and the company suffers financially. If someone has terrific skills and a wealth of knowledge but neglects to show up to use them, that person will be of little value to the employer (and will likely be looking for a new job soon).

Go to work every day and always arrive on time. In fact, report early if you want to make a favorable impression on management. Use the extra time to get organized, review your to-do list, and get a jump on the day's work. Do not worry about coworkers who put in less time—concentrate on building your own career. If you want to get ahead, you must show it.

Companies that have set business hours—whether they are a typical 8–5 work day or three shifts of people working 24 hours a day—expect all employees to follow the rules and work those hours. Some businesses have flex-time, which allows employees to set their own schedules, but they still expect the job to be completed. Make sure you know what your workplace hours are and adhere to your assigned schedule.

Arriving late to work and taking extended breaks day in and day out add up to hours, and eventually days, of missed work. Five minutes here and there may not seem like much until you sit down and do the math. Being five minutes late six times converts to a half-hour of missed work. In less than three weeks, you will have missed nearly an hour.

In addition to being on time, work until the end of your scheduled work day, not a few minutes beforehand. And if you want to make a good impression on management, show a willingness to stay a few extra minutes in order to complete a task or project.

Follow these tips every day:

- Show up every day and do your job.
- Get to work on time and begin your tasks immediately.
- Take the allotted time for lunch and breaks, and make sure you get back to work on time.
- Do not be a clock watcher while you are working.
- Work until quitting time, don't check out mentally a few minutes early.

Sometimes it is necessary to schedule time off work for doctors' appointments, court hearings, jury duty, surgery, etc. If you need to take time off, even if you plan to use a personal day, give as much advanced notice as possible to lessen the inconvenience of your absence. Don't wait until the day before to tell your boss you will be off. If possible, consult with him before making the appointment to see when the most convenient time would be to schedule an absence that you have some control over. If you work closely with someone whose work hours will be affected by covering for you, let her know as soon as possible that you will be taking time off work.

If you do need to take a day off work for sickness or an emergency, follow your company's attendance procedures. Always inform your supervisor right away when you will not be coming in to work for the day. If you are too ill to call, have someone else make the call for you.

 TIP Be on time and return from breaks and lunches as scheduled.

If needed, make sure to present the necessary documentation for missing work (i.e., doctor's excuse, hospital report, court papers, and so on).

13: Be Friendly and Sincere

Smile. It is an outward gesture of happy inner feelings. People will almost always respond well to a smile and will get the impression that you are friendly and helpful, which creates a positive working environment. A smile might even influence a negative situation in a positive way. However, avoid pasting a fake grin on your face, which leads people to believe you are insincere or glossing over their problems.

Greet people with a cheerful "hello" and ask how you may be of service (and mean it!). By sincerely being friendly and helpful, you encourage friendliness in return, minimize conflicts, and develop an "I care" reputation.

Although it may seem you cannot be too friendly to customers, clients, and coworkers, be aware that engaging in long-winded conversations and personal monologues will keep you from completing your duties (and prevent them from completing theirs). Therefore, pay attention to the length of your conversations, and disengage quickly from chat sessions that aren't related to work issues.

Show a genuine interest in people. When you are sincere and make an effort to be friendly, you project an "I care" attitude that makes others more receptive and open. Everyone remembers how they are treated, bad or good, and they often will react in kind.

 TIP | Be friendly, sincere, and honest.

14: Be Honest

Being dishonest is one of the surest ways to sabotage your career and work relationships. Once you are branded as a liar or as someone who cannot be trusted, your reputation is truly damaged. It is difficult to restore trust once it is lost because of lies and deceit. Never deceive others.

Although telling the truth is the core concept of honesty, it encompasses far more. For instance, exaggerating or overstating information, making excuses, cheating, spreading rumors, and falsely blaming others are all forms of dishonesty. Withholding essential facts or not conveying necessary information are also forms of dishonesty.

If it seems as if dishonest people get away with their deceit, know that eventually their actions will catch up with them and turn others against them.

Make sure you communicate honestly with everyone you work with. Take care to provide accurate information to customers, clients, and coworkers. Accurately report facts, costs, delivery dates, and the like. If you do not finish a project on time or if you make a mistake, own up to it and tell the truth.

Be honest with yourself, too, about your own feelings and values. Make a point of being committed to the truth in all your dealings.

15: Admit Mistakes

Everyone makes mistakes. When you make a mistake, it is always the best policy to admit it—right away. Attempting to cover up mistakes, indiscretions, unfinished business, and so on does not change the facts, and will only serve to undermine your employer's trust in you. The truth will always prevail, so just admit the wrongdoing, learn from it, and resolve to avoid that type of mistake in the future. Own up to your actions, face the consequences, and work on a solution. Attempting to cover up even a small infraction undermines your relationships and integrity, and could also prevent the opportunity to fix the mistake and remedy the situation.

Blaming others, making excuses, justifying actions, and ignoring mistakes will only delay their effective resolution and will likely increase any residual fallout resulting from them. In the long run, it is the deception and evasion that will cost you the trust and respect of your supervisor and coworkers, maybe even more than the mistake itself. And if customers and clients are involved, you lose their respect as well. Remember that the mistake you make could have dire consequences for the company, and you may even lose your job, particularly if there is not a swift resolution.

Be careful when attempting to fix a mistake by yourself in the hope that no one will discover you made it. If it is simple enough that you can do it without negative consequences, fine. However, if you make matters worse, the ramifications may also be worse than if you had confessed in the first place and solicited help to resolve the problem.

If you made a mistake and satisfactorily corrected it, you should still tell the boss about it and what you did to correct it. Your admission will help instill a sense of trust and prevent the appearance of a cover-up. It will also give him time to make any adjustments if necessary. Letting your boss know you had a problem but that you figured out a viable solution, shows you are a dedicated worker who can recognize and resolve problems. If you successfully resolved your mistake, it presents an opportunity to showcase your creativity and problem-solving skills.

 Tip _____ Take responsibility for your mistakes and their solutions.

Never unfairly or wrongfully blame others for your own shortcomings and errors. People need to know you are a trustworthy, truthful person who owns up to your own mistakes. Keep your integrity intact.

16: Be Tactful

At times it may be necessary for you to offer criticism, relate negative information, or simply disagree with others. Always do so in a tactful manner by considering the other person's feelings and using professional language, discretion, and good judgment.

Realize the power of words and their impact on the listener. Choose words carefully and avoid negative and personal criticism; negative criticism often elicits defensive and angry behavior, which will only serve to make the situation worse. Make sure your comments are strictly about the work issue, never insult the person, be sarcastic, tell jokes at the expense of others, point fingers, unfairly shift blame, or make inappropriate remarks.

Treat coworkers, customers, and supervisors with respect. Do not rudely boss people around or make unwarranted demands. Make other people feel comfortable by respecting their rights and feelings. It is expected that you will be direct and straightforward when dealing with others, but remain sensitive to their needs. Be discreet.

The next time you are faced with an uncomfortable or difficult situation, think of the tactful way to handle it. Ask yourself these questions:

- How can I relay this information in a polite, respectful manner?
- How would I feel if I were on the receiving end of my criticism?
- Am I acting in a professional manner?
- What is the professional, tactful method of handling this situation?
- Is my tone free of sarcasm, condescension, blame, and anger?
- Are my words professional?
- Have I considered the impact of my words and behavior?

17: Be Confident

It is easy to be confident when you know what you are doing and you do it well. Accumulating success and accolades from management definitely builds confidence. Focus on outstanding performance.

What are your strengths? Being able to perform your tasks efficiently and being knowledgeable about your job leads to confident, optimal performance. How can you build on your strengths and use them to your advantage? Do not limit yourself: think big. By believing in yourself and your abilities, you will increase your self-esteem and self-worth. This in turn will allow you to face new experiences and responsibilities with confidence. Focusing on previous successful accomplishments will boost your confidence and thus enable you to take on greater responsibilities and challenges.

What are some of your past successes? Confidence comes in part from previous accomplishments and the positive feelings they create. Build on those successes. Think of an accomplishment about which you are proud and write it on the line below.

Accomplishment _____

_____

_____

_____

Now answer the following questions regarding this accomplishment:

What did you do to attain the accomplishment?

_____

_____

_____

How did you feel when the accomplishment was achieved?

_____

_____

_____

Can you re-create that accomplishment or a similar one?

_____

_____

_____

What steps can you take toward another successful
accomplishment?

_____

_____

_____

What else can you do to build your self-confidence?

_____

_____

_____

18: Keep Confidences

Much of the information and many of the activities that occur in the office are confidential and should not be discussed with anyone other than those directly involved. It is your responsibility to keep strict confidences and guard business information. Do not intentionally pass along information or let it leak out unintentionally through unsecured files, unmanned computers, overheard conversations, and offhand remarks. Private information, no matter how inconsequential, should be kept private.

Here's one way sharing private information could get you into big trouble:

Sam heard his boss yelling at Alex, another employee, behind his closed office door. From what Sam gathered, the employee had insulted an important customer and possibly lost a huge account. Sam told his friend who works at a rival company how a big account that will affect the company's profitability and stability was lost.

A week later, Sam's boss called him in the office and asked, "What is this I hear about our company going out of business because of losing an important customer?"

Sam stuttered, "I don't know anything about the company going out of business."

"It isn't, but you were the only one within hearing range when I reprimanded Alex for losing us an important customer. Your gossip has now turned into a vicious rumor. We don't need irresponsible, untrustworthy employees in this company."

The message here is never discuss company business with outsiders, particularly with competitors. All client business and information should be treated with the strictest confidence.

Or consider this scenario:

Your friend Helen (a coworker) happened to see a confidential document on her boss's desk that confirmed the transfer to a remote office of Guy (another coworker). At lunch Helen tells you and Stephanie (another coworker) about Guy's transfer. "Guy is going to have a fit when he learns of this transfer," Helen said. "Don't say anything to him, though, because he doesn't know yet."

Later that week Guy goes to Helen's boss and fumes about the transfer he learned about through the office grapevine.

Helen's indiscretion will cost her the boss's trust and cause undue strain and anxiety for Guy and the boss. In addition, Helen learned a valuable lesson about whom she can trust in the office and how comments find their way to the office grapevine.

The question is "Can you be trusted?"

 Keep confidential information to yourself.

19: Be Realistic

Set attainable objectives. Do not subject yourself to unnecessary stress (or the damage to your professional reputation) by over-scheduling or promising more than you can deliver. Be realistic about what you and others can accomplish in a given time period, and don't set unreasonable deadlines. Do not be afraid to ask for help or for a deadline time extension if you can. Your boss will be more likely to offer help and ease the schedule if you are honest about your difficulties and don't wait until the last minute to ask for help. Try to reduce your workload if your schedule is too demanding or impossible to complete.

However, be honest with yourself: Do you really have too much work to do, or are you simply not organized or bad at time management? If you need to improve your skills in order to do your job better, take an appropriate class or seminar. Face the fact that your lack of skills is the problem, not the time you are given to do the task. If your attitude is slowing you down, find ways to improve yourself.

Make sure you have personal time built into your schedule away from work, though. Everyone needs time to regenerate and refresh.

 Be realistic about what you can accomplish so you don't get in over your head.

20: Keep Your Personal Business Out of the Office

It may be tempting to tell coworkers about the big fight you had with your spouse last night, but stop and think about the consequences before you do. How will you feel after you resolve the issue and make up with your spouse, only to have your coworkers think your spouse is the jerk you claimed he was?

What about being drawn into a personal conversation with a coworker friend in which you divulge information about your personal finances that later comes back to haunt you? Suppose your friend spreads your financial information around the office. How will that make you feel? It is a good bet you will feel betrayed, which may permanently impact your friendship and the way you treat the coworker, which in turn will affect the ability of you both to do your jobs well.

Besides losing the respect of your peers and supervisors, bringing personal problems to work creates an uncomfortable working environment for others, wastes office time, and takes your attention away from your job. Most people do not want to be pulled into the middle of someone else's domestic problems, sibling rivalries, financial pitfalls, etc. Discussions of a personal nature have no place in the office, and neither do the bad moods and anger caused by those personal problems. Avoid projecting your mood onto coworkers and customers. Set aside your negative feelings and thoughts, and concentrate instead on the work at hand.

In addition to not divulging personal information, employees should remember that office supplies and equipment are for business, not personal use. Refrain from using telephones, copiers, faxes, and the Internet for personal business except in emergency cases (and make sure to get permission).

The time spent at work when you are being paid by an employer belongs to that employer. That means no personal bill paying, projects, telephone calls, emails, and so forth. When at work, confine activities to work-related business.

Keeping your work life and personal life separate will enhance your professional image and show management that your career is a priority.

Sometimes personal issues (family troubles, terminal illness of a loved one, divorce or separation, death of a family member, volatile disputes, and alcoholism) become an overwhelming challenge that can affect workplace performance. If you find yourself prey to an extremely burdensome problem, talk to your supervisor or a company counselor if one is available. It is crucial to get the emotional support you need so you can find a workable solution.

Some ways of handling these crisis situations include:

- Talk to your immediate supervisor.
- Seek counseling (marriage, alcohol, etc.).
- Face the problem.
- Brainstorm solutions on your own or with the help of other people you trust.
- Reduce your work schedule (part-time, flextime, sabbatical, etc.).
- Use positive self-talk.
- Incorporate healthy habits to take care of yourself (eating right, getting enough sleep, exercising, meditating, reducing caffeine products, etc.).
- Reduce self-pity.
- Write down worrisome problems and some viable solutions.
- Have faith.
- Talk to your doctor.

 Tip Keep personal business to a minimum in the office.

21: Never Discuss Salary with Coworkers

Some salaries are public (political officials, public school personnel) and some are private. Where wages and salaries are confidential, discussions among employees about pay are discouraged (and sometimes prohibited outright) by management because of the negativity such conversations can trigger.

It is amazing how a few dollars' difference in paychecks or how varying raise amounts can cause arguments and hurt feelings. Friendly coworkers can turn on one another over meager amounts that outsiders would think are ridiculous to argue about.

To the people involved in the wage dispute, the disparity represents far more than the actual dollar amount; egos, self-esteem, and self-worth all come into play. For instance, if Tara gets a $.75 raise, but she knows Brittany received $1.00, Tara might question her value to the company, especially if she believes she has performed her job as well as Brittany. Even though the difference in their raises is a mere quarter, it stings to be the one who received the lesser amount. It is tantamount to informing Tara she does not measure up to or is not as capable as Brittany.

In an effort to save face, it is common for an employee who feels slighted to react with statements such as these: "I do more work than Brittany, but I received less money. It is not fair. I break my back for this place, and look how I am treated. Fine. From now on, I'll let Brittany do the work. She's getting all the money." This is a slippery slope that leads to workplace hostility and lost productivity, and it can affect the entire workplace, not just the two people involved.

The bottom line is that no one wants to feel less valuable or less adequate than another person. When two employees perform identical jobs, have the same titles, have been employed with the company for the same amount of time, and appear to be equal in all other regards, they expect equal pay. If one of them learns the other has received a larger raise, problems are likely. It is easy to understand how the employee who receives the lesser raise amount takes it personally, believing she is being unfairly treated and underpaid. The lower paid employee may feel the supervisor thinks the other person is a more valuable worker or worse yet, comes to believe she is a "favorite" of the boss. Even if the higher raise is deserved, the lower paid employee will usually go on the defensive rather than congratulate and be happy for the coworker.

A better course is to simply never discuss your salary or anyone else's with your coworkers.

TIP Discussing salaries in the office is taboo.

22: Use Good Hygiene and Grooming Habits

There are few things worse than working in close quarters with someone who has unkempt hair, dirty nails, soiled clothing, unpleasant body odor, bad breath, and other hygiene indiscretions.

Wake up in time to adequately groom yourself for the day. It seems like common sense; however, at some point we have all encountered a coworker whose hygiene has not met these simple standards. Bathe, wash your hair, and wear clean clothes every day. Use soap, shampoo, toothpaste, mouthwash, and deodorant. Clothes that require dry cleaning should be cleaned and pressed on a regular basis.

Avoid using too much cologne, perfume, and scented hair products or attempting to cover up offensive odors with these products.

Keep your work area clean and odor free and clean up any messes you make in public areas of the company.

TIP Always look your best.

Summary

To make a positive impression on your bosses, coworkers, and customers, display a good work ethic. This necessitates being a self-starter who shows up every day on time, works with confidence and integrity, and displays enthusiasm in actions and speech. Create a positive impact on every person you deal with by keeping confidences, using tact, and avoiding controversies. Develop excellent interpersonal skills and stand out in a responsible, ethical manner.

Everyone appreciates working with friendly, sincere people who are honest and professional in all their dealings. Discussing taboo subjects like salary, breaking confidences, and ignoring personal grooming make negative impressions on people and should be avoided. Avoid bringing personal problems to work, and own up to mistakes you've made and offer to help find solutions.

Chapter 3

Develop Work Savvy

Employers today are searching for, hiring, and promoting intelligent, confident people who possess the knowledge and willingness to do a superior job. These employees also need to be team players and accept personal responsibility for their productivity, decisions, work relationships, and behavior.

Your professional attitude, behavior, and work habits make up your work ethic. If you want to keep the job you have and earn a better one through a promotion or raise, it is imperative to display a professional work ethic.

Doing the minimum required on the job will not get you a title, a corner office, or a bigger paycheck. In fact, you will be lucky to keep a job, particularly in a difficult economy, unless your performance is outstanding and you contribute to the overall success of the company in a positive and visible way.

Work savvy is having an in-depth knowledge of your company and being an expert in your field. The more you understand the operations of the company, the better you can focus on how to apply your special expertise to tasks and problem solving, and the more empowered you become. Mastery of skills crucial to your company and the gaining of specialized knowledge increase your value to the company and secure your reputation as an industry expert. Broadening your industry knowledge, keeping up with leading-edge research, and exhibiting positive work behaviors and performance will give you the leverage you need to have a successful career.

23: Learn About Your Boss

Learning about your boss does not mean delving into his deep, dark secrets, nor does it mean researching his salary and personal spending habits. This research is about taking the time to get to know your boss in a professional sense. What are his credentials, experience, and duties?

Learn enough about your boss to solidify your place on his team. Show an interest in the boss's background as it pertains to the company and his job duties. What exactly does the boss do? Listen to explanations of how routine duties are completed. The more you know about your boss's job and how it is handled, the greater your value to him. Try to figure out how your position supports his.

Even if you cannot perform your boss's duties, knowing something about the work can be a boon whenever you are searching for information or checking and completing documents for him.

How do you go about acquiring information about the boss without seeming as if you are probing for personal information? It depends on the particulars for which you are searching. Through conversations with your supervisor and by reading company newsletters, organization charts, and annual reports, you can learn the answers to the following questions:

- What job-related education does the supervisor have?
- What job-related experience does the supervisor have?
- What degree and/or professional certification(s) does he hold and in what area(s)?
- Does the supervisor have any special skills, especially ones that are strong assets to the company in his particular capacity?
- Where does the supervisor's position fall on the corporate organization chart?
- To whom does the supervisor report and who reports to him?
- Is the supervisor part of a management team? If so, who else is involved?
- How knowledgeable is the supervisor with regard to the company and its products and services?

- What competencies and skills does the supervisor possess regarding his individualized tasks?
- What are the supervisor's routine company-related tasks?
- Does anyone else work closely with the supervisor?
- What special projects does the supervisor work on or supervise?
- How do the supervisor's position and duties fit into the company's overall picture?
- How is the supervisor evaluated and by whom?

The following questions can be answered through conversations with or direct observation of the supervisor:

- What are the supervisor's work habits? For example, is he a purpose-driven workaholic or a procrastinator? Organized or disorganized? Laid back or stressed?
- Does the supervisor allow enough time to meet deadlines or does he work like a maniac to finish at the last possible moment?
- Is the supervisor a competent leader?
- Does the supervisor encourage and motivate employees?
- Does the supervisor communicate clearly?
- What is the supervisor's management style?
- What are the supervisor's strengths? What are his weaknesses?
- What does the supervisor expect from subordinates?
- How does the supervisor evaluate subordinates?

Knowing your supervisor's work habits, expertise, personality traits, and abilities will help you determine the most effective way for you to support him in meeting company goals. This insight will also be valuable overall in forging a better-quality working relationship.

Besides learning about your boss professionally, it is natural that you will gather some personal details in the course of working with him, such as whether he has a family, if he takes cream in his coffee, or prefers danish to donuts.

Consider the following scenario:

> Mr. Saul, the boss, is a procrastinator who lets things go until the last possible minute.
>
> Knowing his penchant for procrastinating, his assistant, Ms. Jist, takes it upon herself to do research for Mr. Saul's current project, to organize the project file, and to set up a timetable for completing the project with time to spare. She then emails him reminders of the timetable deadlines as they approach.
>
> Ms. Jist's friend tells her, "I cannot believe you do Mr. Saul's work for him because he is too lazy to get it finished on time."
>
> Ms. Jist replies, "He is not lazy; he is a busy man. My job as his assistant is to help him get the job done, and that is what I am doing."

Can you see how learning about your supervisor from a professional aspect will benefit you in your position? You can adjust your own work habits and personality to complement the supervisor and increase both your visibility and worth.

Be willing to assume responsibilities you are capable of doing that will lighten the boss's workload and demonstrate your initiative. Sometimes you have to overlook the shortcomings of the supervisor, roll up your sleeves, and pitch in to get the job done.

Learn your boss's company goals, work habits, and background so you can support him.

24: Know Your Company's Products and Services

How can you represent your company or sell customers and clients on your company's products and services if you are unfamiliar with them? No matter what position you hold, you should learn all you can about your company's products and services. Every employee is responsible for sales, because every paycheck depends on whether the company generates income by selling its products and services.

Your willingness to use the company's products and services yourself, if possible, will also go a long way in convincing others that your company delivers quality.

Does your company compile an annual report? Obtain a copy and read it. There is a wealth of information in an annual report besides profit and loss statements. You can learn about the types of products and services your company offers, the types of products that are in the works for the future, the locations of company offices, the number of people employed, the names of the top people in the organization, company expenses, contact information, and so forth.

Does your company produce a newsletter? Consider it a source of insightful and valuable company information and read it thoroughly whenever it is distributed. Pay particular attention to innovations and future plans so that you are always up to date. Contribute articles to the newsletter if you have tips and information to share.

Learn all you can about the company's income-producing business, such as what products the company sells or what services it provides. Be knowledgeable, but never misrepresent yourself or the company. If you do not have information a customer or client wants, know where to turn or who to ask in order to obtain it.

Some other questions to ask:

- What does the company produce, design, manufacture and/or market?
- For what is the product/service used?
- How is the product produced or the service rendered?
- What is the value of the product/service to the customer?
- What are the price, style, dimensions, etc. of what your company sells?
- What new products or services are in the developmental or trial stage for future sales?
- What products or services are being removed from the market or replaced?
- Does the company have product/service quality assurance procedures in place?

- Does the company maintain a high standard for quality?
- Does the company solicit feedback from customers and clients?
- Does the company use customer feedback to improve its products/services?

Learn about the company in general. Although you will want to know about vacation days, benefits, and pay, look for answers to questions such as these:

- What is the company's business plan?
- What is the startup history of the company?
- How many employees does the company have?
- Where does the company have offices?
- Is the company international or domestic? If international, in what countries does the company operate?
- Is the company financially stable? What is the annual sales growth?
- Does the company use the latest technology?
- Does the company have a good reputation in the community (or world)?
- What is the company's standing in the industry as a whole?
- What is the projected growth of the company?
- Does the company have an employee training program?
- How does the company measure quality and performance?
- Is the company privately or publicly owned?
- How does the company contribute to the surrounding community?
- Does the company have plans to expand its office(s)?
- Do employees have opportunities for growth and training?
- Is the company employee friendly?
- Does the company operate with high ethical standards?
- What is the company's reputation for providing customer service?

Learn your company's particular technical jargon or terminology and be able to define the terms. In addition, keep up on industry developments and know the industry lingo and its proper use.

Understanding your company's mission statement and knowing how the company operates will give you a better perspective of how your job fits into the big picture. This will enable you to effectively apply your skills and knowledge, as well as see where you need further development and mastery. Learning about your company's structure will assist you in plotting a path to advancement.

 To best represent your company, know its products and services.

25: Help Your Boss Meet Her Goals

Everyone who is employed has certain tasks or goals to complete at work. The boss is no different than his subordinates in that regard, although some employees feel their supervisors hardly do any work. The truth is the supervisor has company goals that must be met, just like every other employee.

Do you know what your supervisor's goals are? If not, ask her these questions: 1) What are your job-related goals, and 2) how can I help you meet your goals?

It is a fair bet that both you and the supervisor share a unified goal, namely, making the company successful. Success to the boss means staying in business and making a profit. Success to you both means a paycheck and security, among other things.

Keeping the success of the company in mind, find out what your supervisor's goals are with regard to the company and her own job. Those goals should be high priority for your support, and you should direct your energy toward helping to attain them. By looking for ways to help your supervisor succeed, you will also succeed.

Here are some other things to consider:

- What are your supervisor's goals?
- Is there any way you can assist in obtaining those goals?

- Does your supervisor write down goals?
- Does your supervisor use a daily to-do list?
- Does your supervisor follow a set plan of action to achieve certain goals?
- Does your supervisor have a personal mission regarding the company?
- If your supervisor has a mission, does it affect you, your duties, or your position? If so, how?
- How do your duties relate to the boss's goals?

Be proactive. Show an interest in your supervisor's duties, offer your assistance, and be flexible. Are there any tasks you can assume from the supervisor? Clearly state your willingness to learn how to perform the supervisor's routine tasks and to take on additional responsibility in order to alleviate her load. Show initiative by offering assistance with large projects and taking a team player approach.

Of course, make certain you finish your own work on time, or you will undermine your good intentions and possibly anger your supervisor (as well as create more work for her). Be sure the boss authorizes the duties you assume from her and that they are within your responsibility and abilities. Have a clear understanding of where your own duties fit into the overall scheme. Putting the smaller pieces into place can give you a sense of accomplishment.

- What is your role in relation to your supervisor's?
- How does your position contribute to the company's business objectives?
- What impact does your job have on your supervisor's job, your coworkers' jobs, and the company's bottom line?

Be sure to consult with your supervisor on all important projects and tasks, especially those that directly affect the outcome of her work. Sit down with your boss occasionally and discuss your accomplishments to make sure you are meeting or exceeding expectations.

TIP   How can you help the boss meet her goals?

26: Anticipate Your Boss's Needs and Make Yourself Invaluable

How do you anticipate someone else's needs? By paying close attention and staying on top of things. If you can keep a step ahead of your boss by anticipating his needs, you will set the foundation for becoming an invaluable member of his team. Take the initiative instead of waiting for your boss to tell you what to do. What does he need done? Can you do it? Think ahead and be supportive.

No job is too small if it saves the supervisor time. Is there a file you can pull or a call you can return? Can you make copies or send an email or fax? When your boss is inundated with work, can you smooth the way by taking over routine tasks he normally handles?

Pay attention to your boss's work habits. If you understand his style and observe how he handles situations and tasks, you can adapt your own style and also determine where and how best to assist. Keep an eye on your boss's deadlines and schedule. Help define problems and brainstorm solutions. Ask questions and keep the lines of communication clear. The more you know *how* to help your boss, the more valuable you will become.

You can also anticipate on a bigger scale outside of the office. For instance, if you know your boss likes to keep up on the competition, bring relevant articles to his attention. If you hear about customer complaints or suggestions, follow up on them and let the boss know. If you learn of new products or services that will help you and your boss work more efficiently, do some research and present your findings. Bosses are always looking for ways to increase productivity and efficiency while cutting expenses.

TIP Make yourself a valuable member of the boss's team.

Anticipating the Boss's Needs	Yes	No
Do you know what your boss's responsibilities are?	❏	❏
Is your supervisor currently working on a project?	❏	❏
Does your supervisor have an important upcoming meeting?	❏	❏
If a problem arises (with a customer, shipping, production, etc.), can you assist in any way?	❏	❏
Can you compile information or files, do research, or make phone calls for your supervisor without being told what to do or how to do it?	❏	❏
Can you pull related files or contact information for files your supervisor needs to begin a project?	❏	❏
Can you free up time to work on a project for your supervisor?	❏	❏
Are you careful to give complete information when leaving messages?	❏	❏
Can you take on some of your supervisor's routine tasks?	❏	❏
Do you organize documents and files in the way the supervisor prefers?	❏	❏
When completing tasks for the supervisor, do you take into consideration how he prefers the task be done?	❏	❏
Are your tasks current whenever you offer to assist the supervisor?	❏	❏
Do you know your supervisor's work habits?	❏	❏
Do you know your supervisor's preference with regard to running daily operations?	❏	❏
Do you communicate clearly with your supervisor?	❏	❏
Are you flexible when it comes to assisting your supervisor?	❏	❏
Do you periodically review with your boss how you might be of further assistance?	❏	❏
Are you loyal to your boss?	❏	❏

27: Work the Hours Required

Put in the required number of hours you have agreed to work in exchange for a paycheck, and don't try to shortchange your supervisor and company. In fact, if you hope to excel and win a promotion or raise, put in more hours than required. Show up a few minutes early and use the time to plan your day instead of having a second cup of coffee and chatting with a coworker. Be willing to stay as long as it takes to get an important task finished. Spend your time working strictly on business tasks during your required work hours.

Do not take time off unnecessarily. Schedule doctor, dentist, and hair appointments; car and home repair jobs; banking, etc., on your own time when at all possible. It is not your employer's responsibility to give you time off to tend to personal business. Don't abuse sick days by calling off work when you are not sick. Refrain from taking extended breaks and lunches.

If you work from home or another remote location, be sure to work the number of hours that you say you are working. If you are on the company time clock, give the time to the company. Keep a log of the number of hours worked, and hold yourself personally accountable for time owed.

TIP Work when scheduled; be punctual.

28: Pull Your Own Weight

Did you ever work with a slacker—someone who hides when there is work to be done? Have you ever been frustrated waiting for a team member to finish her part of a project so you can do your part? Neither of these types of coworkers makes for pleasant work relations.

Always pull your own weight by completing your duties as efficiently and accurately as possible. Plan carefully and perform consistently. Do what you are supposed to do when you are required to do it. Work quickly and efficiently; show up on time every day. Avoid procrastination. Decide what needs to be done and volunteer to do it.

When you are working as part of a team, make sure you accomplish what is required of you or assigned to you. Meet your deadlines; do not hold team members back when they need your part of the project to finish theirs. When work is divided among employees, do your fair share. Do not rely on other people to contribute time or come up with missing materials that you failed to provide in the first place. Eliminate excuses and avoid waiting and hoping for someone else to do the work. Make team members look competent and support them when they need help. When each individual group member is successful, the entire group succeeds.

Pull your own weight; get the job done.

29: Ask for Help When You Need It

Do not be afraid to admit when you are in over your head. Everyone can use an occasional hand. Discuss your workload with your boss if you are on overload or in danger of job burnout. Ask your coworkers for help for rush jobs and reciprocate at a later date. It is much better to ask for help when you need it than to miss a deadline or fail at a task because you didn't ask for help.

It is impossible to know how to do everything. If you are not sure how to perform duties, find out how they should be done and whether you are completing them correctly. If the job takes two people, ask a team member for help.

You cannot read someone else's mind. If you are asked to do something, make sure to obtain all the necessary information or clarification. Ask questions and keep asking them until you are satisfied that you understand how to do the job. It does no good to play a "guessing game" and guess wrong.

Ask "Why?" Instead of blindly completing tasks, find out what is behind the work you do. Where does the task fit in the bigger scheme? Is anyone else involved? Can anyone else get involved if necessary?

Be absolutely certain about the directions and objectives before beginning a task or project. Ask questions to clarify uncertainties and wait for the answers before proceeding.

Ask for help whenever you are in over your head.

30: Don't be Afraid to Admit You Do Not Have All the Answers

Can anyone really have all the answers all the time? No, of course not.

There is no shame in not having all the answers. The trick is to know where to turn when you need information or whom you should ask. Knowing how to find accurate information quickly is a valuable asset.

For the best results, go to the experts when you need something. If you have to ship a parcel, call a shipping company. If you want the latest employment statistics, go to a government job site. If you need a definition, check a dictionary. If you require help with a computer or software package, contact tech support.

Beware of relying on Internet research when seeking answers. Not all sites provide accurate information, so check your sources carefully.

Keep current reference books relevant to the work you perform in the office. Compile a list of experts you routinely contact.

Know where to find the information you need to do your work efficiently.

31: Don't Bad-Mouth the Boss, Customers, or Coworkers

Making negative comments about the boss, coworkers, and the company are a poor reflection on the speaker as well as the ones the comments are directed toward. Negative comments show disloyalty, immature behavior, unprofessionalism, and poor personal restraint. They also undermine the collective strength of the company team.

Making negative comments about customers undermines the company's reputation and integrity. It erodes goodwill and decreases the ability to sell products and services. If a company's employees bad-mouth customers, those customers will very likely learn of the incidents and avoid doing business in the future. If the comments are made to other customers, those customers may feel they will be bad-mouthed as well. With the loss of trust, there goes customer loyalty.

If you constantly bad-mouth your company or boss, the people you complain to will begin to wonder why you stay in the situation if it is so awful instead of seeking to improve your current situation or looking for another job. Destructive comments create a very negative work environment and poison employees' attitudes. An employee who spreads negativity could face demotion and job loss.

If you feel you have a legitimate complaint, follow the proper channels, bringing it to the attention of your immediate supervisor. If you feel he has not properly handled the grievance, re-state your feelings in a diplomatic manner and tactfully suggest you intend to pursue a satisfactory solution. When you have a legal grievance (sexual harassment, age or race discrimination, disability issues, etc.), contact the proper agencies if the boss does not resolve the matter. Be sure to document the grievance and the steps you took to resolve the problem.

Tip Create a positive work environment; don't bad-mouth anyone.

32: Follow the Company Mission Statement

What the company stands for and believes in is often spelled out in a company mission statement. The mission can be a few words in a slogan or several pages of detailed principles that all employees are expected to follow.

Do you know your company's mission statement? Most companies have one. If your company does, the mission represents your company's ideals. It is the code by which the company operates.

Consider what the mission statement says about the company's values and ethics. How can you, in your day-to-day duties and responsibilities, support and perpetuate the values implied in the mission statement? Do your personal values align with these company values? If not, it will be difficult for you to support that mission.

If your company does not have a mission statement, suggest that employees brainstorm ideas and create one.

Support the values of your company.

Summary

Learning about your boss's goals, background, and work habits positions you to form a better working relationship and assist the boss in meeting his goals. This knowledge will also help you anticipate the boss's needs. Understanding his management style and work habits lets you determine the boss's preferences when it comes to performing tasks. Knowing as much as possible about your company's products and services will allow you to better serve customers and complete your tasks efficiently.

Go to work every day on time. Perform your job efficiently in accordance with the boss's and company's goals. When you need help, ask. When you need answers, find out where to get them.

Chapter 4

Build Positive Work Habits

High on employers' wish lists is the goal of recruiting employees who can think for themselves when performing their jobs. They hope to hire people who can read and/or listen to directions, interpret them correctly, and follow them through to completion. They want people who can assimilate information taken in from a variety of sources and turn it into productive work in a timely manner according to the standards and policies of the company. Employers want to hire people who are skilled and industrious and who fit in with current employees.

To build positive work habits, learn to work efficiently, completing jobs quickly and accurately. Follow directions to the letter, taking care to complete each required step and asking questions whenever you do not understand something. By managing your time, staying organized, and refraining from doing personal work on company time, you can assure your employer that you are giving a good day's work.

33: Follow Directions

Following directions is a process that entails reading and/or listening, interpreting, integrating, and taking action. It encompasses everything from heeding a simple directive to sorting through the complicated explanation of a detailed project and making sense of it.

Before starting any task or project, make sure that you have all the information you need to accomplish it. Missing information can cause a breakdown in communication that may lead to incorrect work and loss of business, productivity, and revenue, among other problems.

Listen carefully to oral directions and summarize what you heard, linking the directions to information you already have. Concentrate on written directions, highlighting the main points. Organize the key information from the directions into an outline or a checklist to which you can refer as you work on the task or project. For more complicated tasks, consider doing a project board on which you can display pertinent information, a timeline, and the names of people involved in the project and their tasks. If possible, confer with someone else who has performed the task or with the person who assigned it.

Although you will want to complete your work in a timely manner, do not rush through it. Make sure that you do not skip a step or misread an important direction. Pay attention to every detail, even if it seems insignificant to you. The smallest missing step could cause the biggest headache in the long run.

If you are given detailed and complicated directions, write them down so that you can refer to them as needed. Keep a copy of directions on file for projects and tasks that are done infrequently—those you only do once or twice a year, such as audits. Writing down directions and keeping them on file will prevent you having to ask for them again, as well as ensure that infrequent tasks are being completed in a consistent manner. In addition, having written directions will help to ensure that you have a clear understanding of the process and goal of your task before you begin, which will in turn make you more efficient in completing your task.

Maintaining accurate written directions for all your tasks also makes you a candidate for training new employees and team members. This show of initiative increases your value to your employer.

Interpreting directions can be difficult when the person giving them is unclear, vague, or gives incomplete information. For example, the person giving the directions may feel she is being clear about what is required. However, the person receiving those directions may get something entirely different out of the conversation, causing poor or erroneous performance.

To prevent misunderstandings and mistakes, immediately summarize what you heard and verify the directions and procedures you were given before you begin the task. Once the job is started, consult with someone familiar with how it should be done, if possible, to make sure you are doing it correctly.

If you are not clear about a point(s) after being given directions, ask for clarification. It makes no sense to do the job wrong, simply because you did not want anyone to know you did not understand the directions or figure out how to do the job.

Learning the *why* behind what you do will help you put the pieces together so they make sense.

Tip   Follow directions to the letter.

34: Don't Gossip or Spread Rumors

The word gossip means idle chat and hearsay. That unflattering definition should be enough to convince you not to participate in gossip. Negative talk about supervisors, coworkers, and customers creates a cynical, distrustful work environment, not to mention the effect it has on productivity. If you are standing around gossiping with coworkers, none of you is doing the job you are being paid to do.

Whether the gossip is true or not is inconsequential. It is unethical and unreliable; professionals should avoid it. Refrain from starting, spreading, or listening to gossip from any source. If others try to engage you in gossip sessions, remove yourself from the situations so that you are not tempted to join in or add to the tales.

People who gossip may have one of several ulterior motives. The gossip could be steeped in retaliation, be a reaction to a negative situation, be a ploy to gain popularity, or be the result of a personality conflict or boredom. Gossipers might genuinely intend to inflict hurt and damage by pitting people against each other, or they may wind up being the unwitting pawns of others. And if people are gossiping with you, they are just as likely to gossip about you to others.

Rumors belong in the same category as gossip. Rumors that cause turmoil and hurt feelings often turn out to be false. You may want to believe a rumor told to you by a trusted friend, but unless the information comes from a reputable source, such as management or the owner, it remains just a rumor. Do not put a lot of faith into it or pass it along to someone else.

Whether based on fact or not, it is never acceptable to add fuel to the fires of rumors by repeating them. In fact, people may believe the person spreading the rumor initiated it. Rumormongers gain a reputation for unethical behavior, causing others to mistrust and avoid them. They may lose integrity, friends, and even their jobs.

A word of caution: If you are not willing to make your comment in public, knowing your boss could hear about it, keep it to yourself. People with integrity are willing and able to stand by their words and actions.

In today's negative economy, it is smart to avoid passing on doom and gloom gossip. Economic and job market realities are negative enough right now. It is senseless to magnify these problems with conjecture and rumors that will cause morale to plunge.

TIP ── Gossip and rumors create a negative work environment.

35: Give a Good Day's Work

While you are at work, do your work, and give it your full attention and effort. Complete assigned tasks with efficiency, accuracy, and expediency. Keep interruptions you can control to a minimum. For example, instead of wasting time grumbling about how much you have to do, just dig in and start working. The time you spend complaining is better spent working on the task at hand. Likewise, avoid complainers or let them know you are busy working. Tactfully encourage them to use their time working.

Periodically assess your performance and how well you complete your tasks to determine if there is a way to increase your productivity or perhaps eliminate nonessential or redundant steps. Track where your time is spent and employ appropriate time management techniques.

Observe others who do similar jobs and compare your productivity to theirs. Is there a way to measure your output against workers in similar jobs? Do you accomplish more than they do? Are you as accurate as they are? Remember, your goal should be to surpass your supervisor's expectations, and one way you do that is by exceeding other employees' output. Pay particular attention to successful coworkers and supervisors. How do they meet their goals, quotas, and deadlines? Can you follow their example? What can you learn from them?

There will be days you may feel tired, irritable, or bored. The professional moves past these feelings to continue performing his job to the best of his ability.

In any economic climate you need to make yourself as useful as possible and avoid giving the impression you are a complainer. You may even be called on to pick up additional work if coworkers are laid off or to reduce your hours and wages to prevent downsizing at your company.

 Make yourself as useful as possible.

36: Be Flexible

The best laid plan can go awry, and you need to be able to adapt—sometimes at a moment's notice. Whenever possible, build a cushion of time into your deadlines, and be willing to switch directions if necessary. Unexpected things have a way of cropping up when you least expect it. It is rare to never incur interruptions on the job. Train yourself to stop and restart tasks with ease and learn to multitask.

Plan, prepare, and organize to the best of your ability, but be flexible with your job duties, bosses and coworkers, time, ideas, performance, and opinions.

Be flexible when carrying out your duties. Look at *how* you do your work and whether it would be better to do it another way.

Flexibility can also mean being pulled from your current tasks to help someone else or having to do something outside your typical job description. With downsizing, job descriptions are often tossed out in favor of "if something needs to be done, do it." No boss wants to hear someone say "that's not my job." Everyone needs to pitch in when necessary. In addition, let go of the mentality "we always do it this way." Instead, accept that things are not always going to be done your way, especially if there is a better way.

A willingness to come in to work early or stay later on occasion to finish projects and tasks is likely to catch the attention of management, as well as allow you to meet deadlines easier.

TIP   Make adjustments as the need arises.

37: Be Efficient

A constant question should be running through your mind while completing your daily tasks: Is there a less expensive, faster, or better way to perform my job? Efficient people constantly evaluate their current methods and procedures, and whenever applicable, they employ streamlined, updated ways of doing the same old job.

Larger, difficult tasks generally warrant extra planning. Before proceeding with a complicated project or task, ask yourself the following questions:

1. Have I considered all the angles to performing this task?
2. Can I complete the job correctly on time?
3. Do I get organized before I begin a task?
4. Do I remain organized while doing my job?
5. Am I competent and resourceful?
6. Do I consider the most cost-effective, time-effective methods for completing my work?
7. Is the tried-and-true method the best way to handle this job?
8. Is there a more effective way of performing my duties?
9. How can I work smarter?
10. Do I waste company time?

The answer to Questions 1 through 6 should be yes. If you did not answer yes, consider how you can become better organized (and take a look at #38). If you answered yes to Question 7 and no to Questions 8 and 9, use the tried-and-true method. If you answered no to Question 7 and yes to Questions 8 and 9, find a more effective method. If you answered no to Question 10, you are on the right track.

Staying on task as long as possible will increase your efficiency and speed, because it takes time to acclimate when switching back and forth between tasks. However, in today's workplace, the ability to multitask is a must as there are priority calls and emails to respond to, meetings to attend, customers to help, etc. Many tasks will not be completed in a single day, but breaking them down into chunks could help you gain blocks of concentration time to aid efficiency.

 Efficient people perform their jobs in a cost-effective, time-efficient manner.

38: Get Organized

Some people seem to have it all together from the moment they come into work; others may putter around and waste the first or last hour or two of the day. An organized mind and work area can make a critical difference in your ability to complete tasks accurately and on time. If you have to spend time looking for files, prices, accounting information, dates, tools, supplies, and so on, it wastes time that could have been spent working on the task at hand. If, however, you have everything you need organized and readily available, you can get started immediately and completely devote your time and attention to accomplishing your tasks. Being organized also cuts down on stress, worry, and irritation because you will not have to stop in the middle of things to search for what you need. In situations where you have to switch between projects or change deadlines, being organized will make it easier to analyze your current situation and predict the impact of changes on the final outcome. Good organization suggests to your boss that you have control over your work responsibilities and can respond to his priority requests.

Unfortunately, being organized does not assure that you will not have any problems, but it will definitely help you assess the "damage" and figure out how to fix it.

Take a few minutes each night before you leave the office or job site and think about the following day's tasks and priorities. Mark calendar appointments, make a to-do list, prepare for upcoming meetings, file last-minute paperwork, and so forth. Planning ahead and knowing what you need for future tasks and projects lays the foundation of organization and will set the tone for your day when you return to work.

TIP   An organized mind and work area puts you in control.

39: Manage Your Time

How well do you manage your time? Do you know for sure where your hours are spent? Do you get the most out of every minute of your day? To find out, keep a journal of how you spend your time for, say, one week. Make a list of the tasks you routinely perform each day and record the time you spend on each. Make sure to account for every minute you can (including all this keeping track of time). Add to the list any weekly or monthly duties and maybe even one-time projects you anticipate, and estimate the time you will spend on these tasks and projects.

Next, track your non-work related time. How much time do you spend away from your tasks? Consider breaks, lunches, meetings, conversing with coworkers and customers, making and receiving phone calls, sending and answering emails, and any other downtime that takes your attention away from your job.

Make an honest assessment of where your time goes while at work, accounting for the minutes as well as hours. Time has a way of slipping away when you are not careful to manage it.

Employers increasingly look for ways for people to work smarter and do more in less time. Keeping a time journal could really help your productivity. In addition, discussing your journal with your boss could present a leadership opportunity to inspire coworkers to try journaling.

Track Your Time

Tasks	Approximate Completion Time
Daily/Routine	_____
Once a Week	_____
Once a Month	_____
Special Projects	_____
Unexpected priority work	_____

Interruptions	Approximate Time
Breaks/Lunches	_____
Meetings	_____
Phone calls	_____
Research	_____
Email	_____
Unexpected conversations with coworkers and customers	_____
Miscellaneous	_____

More Time Management Tips

- When you know you have an extensive project or task due, pace yourself by setting up a timeline if one is not given to you.

- Break large jobs down into manageable increments and plot them on your timeline (doing this will also help you be more organized).

- Build in a cushion of time in case you get interrupted or are pulled away to another project or task.

- Create and use a to-do list.

- Look for creative ways to shave minutes off tasks you do repeatedly.

- Use an electronic calendar to track meetings, appointments, and deadlines.

- Avoid timewasters such as gossiping and idle chatting.

TIP   Know where you spend your time.

40: Do Not Abuse Office Equipment or Take Office Supplies

Company equipment, supplies, and property are not intended for employees' personal use. Even inexpensive supplies, such as pens and paper, are to be used for company business, not home or personal use. Don't walk away with coworkers' pens and supplies.

Treat office equipment with the same regard as you would your own. To avoid excessive repair and replacement costs, follow proper operating and maintenance directions. Every employee is responsible for the proper care of equipment, tools, and property she uses. If you have the additional responsibility of maintaining equipment beyond normal use, follow the appropriate guidelines and schedules.

When sharing peripheral equipment and lunchroom appliances, leave the surrounding area neat and clean for others. If the copier, fax, or printer jams or runs out of paper, do not walk away and leave the problem for the next person. Figure out how to remove the jam and re-fill the paper. Re-stock incidental supplies in common areas. Courtesy goes a long way in keeping the peace when sharing equipment and space.

TIP   Every employee is responsible for the proper care of company property.

41: Avoid Using Office Phones for Personal Business

Company telephones are for business, not personal, use. The phone lines should be kept free so that you and your customers, supervisors, and coworkers can conduct company business. Making and receiving personal calls at work not only ties up the telephone lines, but also costs the company in higher phone charges, unproductive work hours, and lost business. Companies pay their employees to work. It is not fair or reasonable to expect wages for time spent on personal business.

Most supervisors realize that employees have lives outside of work and are not opposed to employees' receiving emergency calls, but they are against abusing phone privileges. Some companies may even track phone usage and monitor calls.

Never, never let a customer stand and wait while you are conducting personal business.

42: Avoid Wasting Company Time on Personal Interests

Sending and receiving personal texts, whether by cell phone, Blackberry, or computer, is basically the same as making and receiving personal phone calls during work hours. Everything you do on company time affects your productivity. Stay on task, and keep it professional. With people working longer hours, it is acceptable to make quick phone and email reservations, appointments, and the like while at the office. The key is to use discretion, to be brief, and to return 100% of your attention to your job. Avoid spending half the morning playing online games and writing lengthy personal emails. Keep in mind you have a moral obligation to give your employer a fair return on his wages.

43: Avoid Wasting Company Time on the Internet

Although the Internet has become an essential tool of business today, many companies block its use because of employee abuse. Unfortunately for employers, the Internet has become an integral part of their employees' personal lives with the wide availability of websites, social sites, email accounts, forms of instant messaging, and general knowledge sites. It is easy for employees to spend far too much company time on personal Internet use. Many of these employees then complain they do not have time to finish their work or they are overloaded. They do not consider a few minutes on the Internet to be a problem. However, those minutes quickly add up to hours.

Most companies are adamant about restricting employees from accessing risqué and/or illegal Internet sites. Employees caught scouring such sites may quickly find themselves out of a job. Employers can and do aggressively monitor their employees' email accounts and Internet access.

Employers may review Internet browsing histories and dismiss employees for infractions such as viewing sites with inappropriate sexual content, which can be considered sexual harassment or creating a hostile work environment. Email and Internet access in the workplace is NOT considered private by law. Companies are within their rights to view their employees' email and Internet activity, and they can and will fire you if inappropriate, illegal, or offensive information is found. Your company's IT or HR department may be in charge of constantly monitoring emails and Internet histories.

If the Internet is available at your company, use it for business purposes ONLY.

 Use your phone, email, and Internet as if they are being monitored by your employer.

44: Do Not Complain

Enthusiasm is contagious; unfortunately, so is complaining. Would you rather be around an enthusiastic person or a complainer? Obviously, someone who is enthusiastic will make your workplace more pleasant.

If you do have a legitimate problem or complaint, you should try to propose a solution when you bring it to the attention of someone who can do something about it. This will help you project an image of being a problem-solver instead of a complainer, and also show that you are invested in the success of your business or workplace.

Avoid constant complainer mode by searching for the positive aspects of any given situation. Chronic complainers gain an undesirable reputation by darkening the atmosphere and undermining morale.

Identify what frustrates you and then sit down and think about ways you can make improvements. Is there something you can do on your own to resolve the situation? If it is within your authority and responsibility, do it. Research similar problems and find out how they were handled. Would the resolution used on a similar problem be a viable option for handling your complaint?

Can you brainstorm solutions with your coworkers? Do you think it will help to speak with a supervisor about your complaint? If, after presenting the situation to the supervisor, you learn nothing can be done to resolve it, you must find a way to let it go and put it out of your mind. Instead, concentrate on the positive aspects of your job, or at least work on improving the negative things that are within your ability to change.

An economic downturn and fear of layoffs and company closings can place undue stress on employees who are concerned about keeping their jobs. Negative comments and complaints only heighten the anxiety and worsen the situation. Therefore, it is critically important to maintain a positive, upbeat attitude.

Avoid making negative comments and complaints in an already pessimistic environment.

45: Do Not Waste Time on Idle Chat

Idle chatting and gossiping cost companies hundreds of hours of productivity. Water fountains, copiers, printers, fax machines, elevators, break rooms, parking lots—anywhere employees gather informally can be problem areas that encourage pointless conversation.

It is easy to fall into the routine of chatting with coworkers about non-business related matters, and although some workplace socialization is beneficial, thousands of hours a year are wasted on trivial conversations that steal company time. Customer service may even suffer when employees ignore customers while they finish personal phone calls or texts. Waiting customers who are on the receiving end of such unprofessional behavior will avoid doing business with the company in the future, and who could blame them?

Another downside of having coworkers congregate and participate in idle talk is that such discussions often evolve into complaint sessions. One disgruntled employee fuels the fires of several others who begin to question things that were not a problem earlier. This negative banter can erode what is an otherwise pleasant atmosphere.

TIP Do not let idle chatting affect your productivity.

46: Write It Down

Who can remember everything? Who wants to remember everything? Why clutter your mind with incidentals or take the chance of forgetting important information?

Write down facts, directions, names, dates, amounts, and the like when it is crucial to remember them. Trusting your memory with vital data leaves substantial room for forgetting and misunderstanding. Even simple information you think you will be sure to remember can slip your mind given the right circumstances. Why take a chance?

Keep a notebook handy or use a computer file to write down directions and the steps to complicated procedures. Create to-do lists and leave sticky notes as reminders of things to do. Write down the complete details of phone messages, including the date, time, name of the person/company, and a summary of the call.

If your boss gives directions, grab a pen. If the telephone rings, pick up a pen and paper before answering.

TIP If it is crucial to remember something, write it down.

47: Produce Error-Free Work

Double-check all facts, figures, dates, names, addresses, locations, and times. Proofread carefully, and do not become reliant on spell check and grammar check. Those computer applications are convenient, but they are not perfect.

Employees whose work is inaccurate cost their businesses time, money, and goodwill. They decrease their effectiveness and overall personal worth to the company. Mistakes tarnish a work record and a reputation. Mistakes put the company in jeopardy due to lost revenue, time, labor, confidence, customers, productivity, and more.

Your priority should be to produce error-free work on a consistent basis. Quality should take precedent over speed. If a job is incorrect, it doesn't matter how quickly you did it. Erroneous work benefits no one; rather, it is a waste of time and assets.

Be especially diligent when checking amounts and figures; an extra zero or decimal point out of place can be a disastrous, costly mistake your company may not be able to recover from easily. Verify dates so that important deadlines and meetings are met. Check names and addresses to ensure that information reaches the proper people and places in a timely manner. It is annoying to the receivers to open documents with their names spelled incorrectly and to have to wade through typos and incorrect information. Typos certainly send the wrong message. Informal in-house correspondence such as emails and memos to coworkers should be just as error-free as documents going outside the company.

When you produce accurate, efficient work, it is not only a reflection of you, but also a reflection of your employer. Make the employer proud that you are on the team. Think quality in every job you do.

TIP Accuracy is a top priority.

48: Consolidate Tasks

Consolidating similar tasks can be a timesaver. For example, consider the simple task of writing a letter: compose, type, and print a letter; make copies of attachments; type and print the envelope; fold and insert the letter into the envelope; run the envelope through the postage meter; and drop the letter in the outgoing mail. If you have several letters to do, would it save time to compose all of them at one sitting? If you have a couple of hours to concentrate, you may be able to accomplish more and better compositions (and if they are similar letters, you might be able to avoid re-typing each one by using a generic boilerplate or template and simply changing specific details). Then you could type, print, and post all of the documents in the same time period rather than doing a letter here and an envelope there, making a copy here and filing it there before starting the process again.

Is it possible to return several phone calls in the same hour instead of making a call, doing a different task, making another call, and so on?

TIP Save time—consolidate similar tasks.

49: Manage Stress

Fast-paced workplaces combined with equally fast-paced personal lives create stress overload. Stress overload on the job leads to poor performance, mistakes, forgetfulness, strained relationships, health problems, and more. Workplace stress can affect an employee's personal life negatively. Conversely, personal life stresses negatively affect workplace performance. In this day and age, it is impossible to avoid stress, which makes it critically important to find ways to manage stress so that your workplace performance and relationships are not adversely affected. Some of the best stress busters include eating healthy foods, getting regular exercise, and getting adequate sleep.

Many nutrition magazines and websites are devoted to planning healthy, balanced meals. You can also check government websites for nutrition, exercise, and sleep guidelines. Health insurance companies provide a wealth of information to their enrollees through their websites and the distribution of printed materials and email. Ask your company's cafeteria personnel or vending machine company to provide healthy food alternatives and snacks. Substitute water for sodas and caffeinated drinks.

Begin or resume an exercise program after checking with your doctor, who can also provide nutrition information. Does your company have an exercise room or offer gym memberships or participate in other types of exercise plans? Does the company have a softball team or can you organize one? Ask coworkers or friends to go for a walk during your lunch break a few times a week. Instead of riding the elevator up or down a floor or two, take the stairs. Take advantage of opportunities to move and get your heart rate up during the day—doing so will help to relieve stress and clear your mind.

Discuss difficult workloads and projects with your supervisor before you reach the burnout stage. Resolve conflicts with coworkers and make up your mind to avoid negative people as much as possible.

During difficult economic times, make a real effort to remain optimistic. Find ways to reduce your stress level, perform your job to the best of your ability, and avoid negative people. Stay on top of the latest developments in your field and keep your resume, portfolio, and skills updated.

Manage your stress so it does not affect your workplace performance.

Stress Reduction Tips

- Make up your mind to look on the positive side.
- Develop a routine and stick to it.
- Keep your workstation and work life organized.
- Arrange your work area to minimize interruptions from others.
- Get up and take a quick break when you start to feel overwhelmed or tired.
- Talk things over with a trusted colleague or supervisor when you start to feel stressed.
- Make and follow a to-do list, concentrating on the most important tasks first and working your way through the list in priority order.
- If a big job gets overwhelming, take a break from it and work on an easier task.
- Break down large projects into smaller, more manageable tasks.
- Take the breaks, lunches, and vacations to which you are entitled. You will perform better and more efficiently if you take a break and relax every once in awhile.
- Be flexible and resilient.

- Have fun (read, play sports, go for a hike or to the theater or a park, etc.).

- Maintain a sense of humor.

- Exercise—consider exercises you can do while sitting at your desk or performing your duties.

- Eat healthy foods and snacks. Avoid the vending machine unless healthy snacks and drinks are stocked.

- Bring a reusable water bottle to work and refill it often.

- Get enough sleep every night and stick to a regular sleep schedule.

- Maintain a healthy body weight.

Summary

Positive work habits increase productivity and enhance workplace relationships. Give your employer your best every day by producing error-free work in an efficient, timely manner. Follow directions carefully, writing down crucial information. Set up a system for staying organized and managing your time, but remain flexible. Even the best laid plans can change. Create a positive work environment by maintaining an upbeat mood and optimistic outlook. Avoid complaining, idle chatting with coworkers, gossiping, and activities that poison the workplace environment and take time away from your duties. Incorporate stress-reduction techniques into your daily routine, especially during difficult times, and encourage coworkers to do the same.

CHAPTER 5

SKILLS AND EDUCATION

Accprding to the Bureau of Labor Statistics website (http://www.bls.gov/emp/emptab7.htm), people with advanced degrees can earn more than twice as much as those with high school diplomas.

Higher education is an investment that pays big dividends. Advanced degrees and continuing education pave the way for better opportunities, more successful careers, higher salaries, and greater job satisfaction. Educated employees make better decisions and are generally more self-confident and articulate.

If you work in a position or an industry that does not require a degree, check to see if you can increase your professional worth through certifications. Many industries provide certification for expert level attainment of a particular skill or knowledge area. If your position does not require a degree or certification, it is still advisable to keep skills current and polished, as well as to strive to increase your overall industry-related knowledge.

Your education does not stop when your formal education stops. Commit to lifelong learning. In today's workplace environment, there is no way around it. Get as much education and training as possible to help you perform better in your current position and increase your marketability. Investing in yourself through education is one of the most rewarding things you can do to challenge yourself and to position yourself for promotions and better job opportunities. Education also protects you from unemployment by increasing your value to your company and also making it easier for you to market your skills outside your current job. In addition, if you learn new sought-after skills, you will be able to draw on them to gain promotions or other employment.

50: Keep Up to Date

Becoming outdated is a sure way to cut your career short. You will remain marketable by not only maintaining your present competencies but also learning new ones. Skill maintenance is an ongoing process, especially with changing and evolving technology, new research and development, and modernized equipment. These and a number of other variables can make the skills you have today outdated or obsolete tomorrow. In addition, ever-changing job descriptions, procedures, tools, and so on affect what and how much you need to know and how well you perform your job overall.

Competencies that you might consider achieving are oral and written communications, customer service, marketing, sales, and computer software skills to name a few. These abilities are valued in a number of jobs and industries.

To determine the best way to update your skills, (1) review your job description and verify the core competencies and skills you need in your current position, (2) make a list of competencies and skills required for you to perform your job and assess your degree of competency in each, (3) ask your supervisor if he feels there are competencies and skills you need to acquire, and (4) ask coworkers, the human resource director, and/or your company trainer if there are competencies or skills you should acquire in order to increase your value to the company.

After you have a good idea of what competencies and skills you need, answer these questions:

- What are your current strongest competencies/skills?
- What competencies/skills do you need to improve or expand?
- Have coworkers, your supervisor, or company trainer pointed out competencies/skills you should acquire to increase your value to the company?

- How will you obtain the training you need? When will you do it?
- How will you know if you have achieved your training goal?
- If you gain additional competencies/skills, how will you benefit?
- Are there additional competencies/skills you can obtain that will prepare you for another position or advancement?

After assessing your skills and competencies, determine which ones you need to update your current skills and which new ones will improve your marketability in the industry. Then, write a professional development plan that includes the following:

- A list of the skills/competencies that will be beneficial to you on your present job and to attain future advancement
- A skill/competency to begin your training chosen from the list you created
- The date by which you will obtain the training
- Where you will obtain the training
- Some form of measurement to assess if you have attained the competency

 TIP Obsolete skills and knowledge will cost you your job.

51: Learn from Your Mistakes

If you think you are beyond making mistakes, think again. Everyone makes mistakes. It doesn't matter how skilled or experienced you are; if you are human, mistakes will happen. Successful people assume responsibility for their mistakes and turn them into learning experiences.

If you make a mistake, find out exactly what you did wrong and determine whether there is a way to fix the problem. Brainstorming solutions increases your creativity, improves your judgment, and enhances your reputation as someone who can come up with viable answers when necessary.

Most importantly, make sure you learn something from the mistake. Determine why or how you made the mistake and what you need to do differently in the future so that you will not make the same mistake again.

Here are some questions to ask yourself when you make a mistake:

- Did you admit your mistake? If not, why?
- Did you brainstorm ideas for correcting the mistake? If not, why?
- Did you offer solutions? If not, why?
- Did you implement corrective solutions? If not, why?
- Did your solution work? If not, did you look for other solutions?
- What did you learn from the mistake that will help you develop better judgment?
- If someone else shared responsibility for the mistake, what did you learn from that experience?
- How can you avoid making a similar mistake in the future based on what you have learned?
- Do preventative measures need to be put into place?
- Are you able to implement changes so that the mistake will not be repeated?
- Are you able to help others avoid making a similar mistake?

If you learn something from a mistake you make and develop better judgment for handling similar situations, the experience takes on a positive spin. Develop a workable plan to help you avoid similar mistakes and then implement appropriate changes to prevent future mistakes. Your handling of a mistake impacts how others perceive you professionally. Everyone makes mistakes, but it is important not to blame someone else, overreact, or hide the mistake. If you remain calm, accept responsibility, and offer to help resolve the mistake, others will perceive you as responsible, level-headed, and honest. Your creative brainstorming of solutions also provides a leadership opportunity where a mistake had been.

TIP   Your handling of mistakes impacts how people perceive you professionally.

52: Learn Something New Each Week

To keep your mind fresh and open to new ideas, try to learn something new every week. This can be done in a formal or informal setting. There are lots of ways to accomplish this.

Ask your supervisor for an explanation of why the tasks and projects you complete are important. Where do they fit into the company's overall operations? Why are they done a certain way? What policies drive them? Can they be streamlined to increase your productivity?

When you attend meetings, pay particular attention to information that relates directly to your position and duties. Think about how the information can help you do your job more effectively. Listen also to information that may not be directly related to your job as you might acquire some useful tips you can transfer to your own responsibilities. Be open-minded when ideas are proposed. Even if the idea does not pertain directly to you and your job, there may be a way the idea can be adapted to your situation. You may be able to adapt someone else's idea to fit your circumstances.

When engaged in casual business conversations, even around the water cooler, listen. You never know when someone will suggest an idea that you can apply to your job or that will spark a comparable idea in your mind. A casual comment could turn out to be the solution you have been seeking. Engage in conversations with coworkers who are more intelligent and experienced than you are. Ask questions to absorb some of their knowledge. Associate with other people who like to learn and trade ideas.

What you learn for the week does not necessarily have to be academic or even job related. You can learn personal skills that will help you get along with coworkers or relate to customers and clients. You can learn something fun just to keep your mind agile. You might learn a new exercise technique, cook a new recipe, or learn the rules to a new card game. The possibilities are endless.

Here are some other ways to learn new things:

■ Join professional organizations that teach skills through workshops and speakers (Toastmasters, Women in Business, Sertoma, and college and fraternal organizations).

- Subscribe to and read magazines in your profession so you can stay in touch with the latest trends.
- Research online companies that offer products or services similar to yours.
- Research online to find better ways to perform your job duties (i.e., organization and time-management tips, new product developments, and so on).
- Listen to coworkers explain how they solve various work-related problems.
- Listen to customer/client feedback.
- Ask coworkers about their jobs and how they perform their tasks; be attentive.
- Listen to news program segments about product development.
- Read a good newspaper.
- Thoroughly read your company's newsletters.
- Read newsletters published by other companies who offer products or services similar to yours.
- Read online e-zines and informational blogs pertaining to your field or skill area.
- Do something you have not done before (i.e., learn another language, build a computer, parachute from a plane, etc.).
- Always be on the lookout for information you can use.
- Search for ways to make your job more challenging or more effective.

A wealth of information is contained right in your company files. Learn as much as you can about your company and its products and services. Although you do not want to rummage through confidential materials, the general files can provide the following useful information:

- Customer/client names and business contact information.
- Customer/client purchasing information—what products and services they use on a continuous basis.
- Products and services your company offers and information about them.
- New product and service developments.

- To whom the bulk of your company's products and services are sold.

- Sales and marketing figures.

- Minutes from previous company meetings.

 TIP Each day presents endless learning possibilities.

53: Improve Your Skills

Skills improve with use, but over time, some will become outdated and unused ones can become rusty. Take personal responsibility for keeping your skills up-to-date. Sharpen your skills to increase your value to your company and give you an edge in your field. Look for upcoming industry trends and investigate the types of skills that you will need to stay ahead of those trends.

Computer skills are always worth updating, especially software programs used often in your field. If you do not utilize computer technology in your current position, consider enrolling in computer classes anyway. The courses could make you indispensable if your company updates its technology or ease your transition to another company, not to mention make you a candidate for other jobs in your company that require those skills. Think of ways you can use technology at work and in your personal life so that you can practice and retain what you learn in your classes.

One way to improve skills is to use them on a continuous basis, because skills are enhanced through repetition. Another way to increase and/or retrieve lost skills is to take a skill development course. There are many avenues for taking courses ranging from formal classroom settings to seminars to online classes to apprenticeships. It does not matter how you gain the skills; it only matters that they are well developed and used on a regular basis.

Many skills can be learned or improved in your own home. For instance, if you need to learn to type or increase your typing speed and accuracy, purchase a home typing program or practice on a free or paid online site. If you want to improve your marketing skills, read marketing books.

Some government employment agencies, libraries, and temporary agencies offer free skill courses. High schools, vocational schools, and community colleges offer courses in everything from computer training to car repairs at reasonable rates.

Routinely assess your skills to make sure you have what it takes to get the job done in a timely, effective manner. Look for ways to gain cutting-edge skills in your particular field.

TIP Keep skills honed and learn new ones that will increase your value.

54: Keep Up with Technology

It is a given that technology will continue to change and evolve. When dealing with and using technology on a regular basis, it sometimes seems an impossible challenge to keep abreast of changes and updates. To be effective and stand out in the workplace, you should complete the latest computer and technology training in your industry.

Even if your company cannot take advantage of new technology now, it is preferable to read about and research innovations, new theories, and methods of operation. Why should you bother learning about technology your company does not use? Many of your company's customers and clients may be familiar with or use the newest technology in their businesses. If you are at least familiar with the technology they use, you can carry on a knowledgeable conversation and determine how to better fit your services to their needs. Additionally, your company may update technology at some point; you would be in a position to provide assistance with the selection of proper equipment and the implementation of new programs and technology into current workplace processes if you have studied what is available. You could even help train people to use the new technology.

Knowledge of the latest technology could make you a very valuable asset if the new technology will require fewer employees (i.e. not as many people required to do the job). If you already know the technology, you will be in a better position to keep your job over employees who do not.

Change and evolve with new technology.

55: Keep Up with Advancements in Your Field

Staying on top of the latest developments in your field increases your value to your company in many ways: (1) you know what competitors are doing, (2) you can provide input into what your company should be doing to remain competitive, (3) you can get ideas for new product development and ways to offer and market your services, (4) you are better aware of new trends and practices that can impact your company's performance and your own job performance (and job security), (5) you stand out among your peers, and so forth.

How can you keep up with the latest developments? By doing the following:

- Attend conferences and seminars
- Enroll in classes
- Read trade journals
- Attend trade shows
- Do online and library research
- Participate in coworker discussions

Regularly read literature, magazines, and journals that inform you of market trends and economic news in your field. You can determine how your company fits in with others in the industry or learn about opportunities other companies offer. Knowing what competitors are doing can help you stay competitive, as can knowing about current and forthcoming products and services in the field. Trade journals are specific to certain industries and detail developmental trends and industry knowledge in those fields. There are trade journals for dozens of industries. Choose one devoted to your field and search through it for tips.

To stay competitive, keep up with advances in your field.

56: Take Classes or Attend Seminars and Lectures

Professionals who want to improve their skills and keep up with the latest developments and knowledge in their field often take appropriate courses through community colleges, vocational schools, nonprofit organizations, professional groups, online learning institutions, and the like. There is a wealth of knowledge to be gained in adult education and career-development classes at these types of institutions.

Continuing education is extremely important. It affects everything from promotions to job retention to lifetime earnings. Decide what you need to learn to remain in your current job or to advance, and then sign up for appropriate classes, workshops, and lectures.

Many companies offer their employees tuition reimbursement for successfully completed classes. If your company offers tuition reimbursement, take advantage of that and any other free or reduced training available from the company. In addition, various loans, scholarships, and grants are available for continuing education. Sometimes classes and workshops are free.

You may even want to ask your supervisor her opinion as to what education and training will benefit you, where you can get the training, and if the company reimburses tuition. Write a proposal to present to your employer stating (1) the education/training that will benefit you in your current job, (2) where you can receive the education, (3) when the class or training begins, (4) how the company will benefit, (5) the cost, and so on.

If the company does pay tuition reimbursement, talk to human resources to find out what preliminary paperwork must be completed, what the requirements are (i.e., maintaining an A or B in the class), how much is reimbursed, and how the reimbursement is paid (to you directly or to the school; in one lump sum or in payments).

Even if you don't have access to free or reduced classes, investing in your education can pay big dividends compared to the cost. An education is something that cannot be taken away from you no matter what happens in your future. Your education can see you through difficult economic times, a poor job market, and a layoff. When you have a solid education, you can negotiate higher starting salaries, better benefits and perks, raises, and take advantage of advancement opportunities. Many companies, through their employee evaluation and review processes, require that employees set goals to be completed for the next evaluation (i.e. obtaining certifications or continuing education units). Completion of these goals often results in job retention, raises, and promotions.

All education and training is valuable, even if it is unrelated to your specific job. You never know what skills will be needed in the future. In addition, consider taking classes just for the love of learning. It is an excellent way to keep your mind sharp and to meet and network with new people in your field who are working in other companies. Developing relationships with like-minded professionals outside your company provides opportunities to learn how other people solve problems and perform jobs similar to yours. Networking with these professionals can also give you a big advantage in job searches.

Classes can be found on anything you enjoy from cooking to sign language to floral arrangements to guitar playing. Thousands of offerings are available in brick and mortar buildings and online. Open yourself to the possibilities, and encourage friends and coworkers to join you. Exercise your brain and creativity.

Some people claim they are overqualified for jobs because of their education. If that is the case, those *overqualified* people might consider applying for jobs suited to their education and experience. Obviously, they are applying for the wrong jobs.

Equate learning with success and advancement.

57: Get a Degree

The Bureau of Labor Statistics indicates that people with degrees make more money in their lifetimes than those without degrees. Advancement opportunities in many companies are often contingent on having an advanced degree. If you are considering attaining a degree, choose an area you are interested in so that you will do well in your classes (as well as enjoy them more). If you are not sure what area you should pursue, talk to trusted friends and family members about their chosen careers and about your particular interests. Consult your employer or human resource personnel, a career counselor, or a college advisor. You can also take a career placement test available online, at many schools and colleges, and through government employment agencies.

So how are you supposed to pay for a degree, which can be expensive? Options may include the following:

- Company tuition reimbursement
- Government training programs
- Corporate training programs
- Government loans and grants
- Individual loans and grants
- Individual and professional organization scholarships
- Scholarships offered through endowments and higher learning institutions
- Reduced or free training offered by professional organizations
- Out-of-pocket money from a job
- Paid internship or apprenticeship

If obtaining a degree does not sound appealing to you, try to motivate yourself by thinking about the personal stake you have in holding advanced degrees and certifications. Believe in your ability to set educational goals and see them through to completion.

How do you find time for school while working full time? If you want to manage your career, you will find time. Nearly half of college students are adult learners who are motivated to work hard and learn all they can. They practice time management to fit in assignments and studying; for example, using breaks and lunches to review class assignments and information. Because of work and home commitments, many attend school part time. Most schools have flexible options for today's busy students, who find ways to adjust even with job and home responsibilities.

If you are worried about having enough time to pursue a degree, look over this list of tips:

- Set learning goals
- Decide what you want to accomplish and draw up a workable plan
- Avoid procrastination; get enrolled
- Sign up for the most convenient classes and times
- Consider the difficulty of courses and the amount of time needed for assignments; ease into learning by taking a less difficult course to begin
- Take refresher courses if needed
- Set aside time for completing assignments and studying
- Make up your mind to get your money's worth by attending every class
- Use resources available to you (tutors, group study sessions, advisors, library, learning center, etc.)
- Take notes in class
- Form study groups
- Find a school friend or mentor
- Address problems immediately
- Delegate household chores
- Prepare and freeze meals on off days
- Say **no** more often when people want your time
- Balance your home, work, and school commitments
- Practice stress reduction, get enough sleep, eat right, and exercise

TIP Make obtaining a degree part of your educational goal.

58: Get Certified

If certification is available in your particular field, you will increase your professional value by getting certified. Be careful of how and where you obtain certification, making sure to use a reputable source. Schools, colleges, and organizations offer certification onsite, in classrooms, and online.

Study materials are available for many certification exams. These materials can increase your chances of passing the certification exams.

Many certifications require the holder to be re-certified periodically (i.e. CPR certification). In such cases, you will want to make a note of the date your certification will become invalid and renew it before that date. When you receive your certification, you will be given instructions on maintaining the certification.

If it increases your value in your field, get certified.

59: Develop Good Judgment

Good judgment comes from trying and failing, gaining knowledge and putting it into practice, repeating tasks, learning from past experiences, and using critical thinking.

The longer you work in a particular job situation, the more familiar you become with the jargon of your particular industry, your company's products, services, clients, and methods of operation. Learning this information will hone your judgment skills.

The more decisions you make and outcomes you experience, the better you can judge outcomes in similar instances. Of course, you may not always be correct in your decisions or assumptions, but it certainly helps to have past experiences to guide you. Treat all your experiences as learning opportunities. As stated previously, your mistakes will aid in the development of good judgment.

Learn something from everything you do; every opportunity is a learning opportunity.

Summary

Education and skill development should be top priorities if you hope to keep your job and possibly advance. Outdated skills and knowledge can quickly become a liability in an economy where layoffs and downsizing are prevalent. Learn something new every week from colleagues, classes, customers, and even your mistakes. Keeping up with technology and advancements in your field increases your value, as does receiving certifications and degrees. Assimilate all your learning, education, and experiences so as to develop good judgment and your area of expertise.

CHAPTER 6

FOSTER PEOPLE SKILLS

If you have a job, you undoubtedly have to deal with people in some capacity—customers, coworkers, or supervisors. By applying positive, professional human relations skills in your dealings with others, you will increase your worth to any company for which you work. It is critical to give serious attention to this important area of your work life. Always remember there are plenty of other people who are ready to satisfy your boss and your customers if you do not. And if you cannot get along with coworkers, you could quickly become a liability to your employer.

People Skills Rating

	Always	Sometimes	Rarely
I enjoy meeting new people.	❏	❏	❏
I am friendly toward new people I meet.	❏	❏	❏
I am confident when meeting new people.	❏	❏	❏
I am good at solving problems.	❏	❏	❏
I remain calm under pressure.	❏	❏	❏
I am a good listener.	❏	❏	❏
I think before speaking.	❏	❏	❏
I am articulate.	❏	❏	❏
I learn all I can about my company and its products and services.	❏	❏	❏
I respond with tact and professionalism in difficult situations with others.	❏	❏	❏
I do my job with a high degree of accuracy and efficiency.	❏	❏	❏
I am a team player.	❏	❏	❏

Obviously, the best answer for each of the People Skills Rating items is *always*. Completing this exercise is a good way to discover where your strengths and weaknesses lie. You will then be in a better position to know which traits to improve—those you ranked *sometimes* and *rarely*.

In this chapter, the principal emphasis is on treating others as you wish to be treated. This includes everyone you come into contact with—customers, coworkers, and supervisors. When it comes to customers, provide the best service you can so they keep returning to do business with your company. Get along with your coworkers and boss by treating them with respect and kindness.

60: Provide Excellent Customer Service

Customers generate revenue for a company; without them, there would be no reason for a company to be in business. Each customer has intrinsic value and should be treated with respect and professionalism.

To let customers know you appreciate them, be sensitive to their needs by intelligently and honestly focusing on their concerns. Listen when they talk to you and respond with empathy and understanding. Take nothing about what customers say for granted. Summarize what you heard and repeat it to the customer to be sure you have the correct facts and can address his or her needs. Maintain good eye contact and pay attention to nonverbal cues, which could indicate a discrepancy between the spoken words and actions. For instance, a customer may say a solution is fine but have a puzzled facial expression, which indicates confusion.

Learn what will keep your customers happily returning time and again. Develop a connection with them that strengthens not only your business relationship but also your personal one. Learn the names and preferences of repeat customers. Get to know which customers prefer specific products and services your company offers. Know which customers may need extra care in the way their business is handled. Always be polite. If you do not satisfy your customers, you will find yourself with less and less business.

Be knowledgeable about your products and services. Learn as much as possible so that you can answer customers' questions intelligently and honestly. In fact, be a fountain of information. Try the products and services you promote, read your company's available literature, ask questions of coworkers and the supervisor to be sure of essential points, and find out what facts are important to your customers. If you do not know the answer to a customer's question, find out from someone who does; don't guess or misrepresent the company. Knowledge promotes confidence—both yours and the customer's. In addition to being knowledgeable about your products, memorize your company's policies so that you will know what to do if a customer has a problem.

So what do your customers want? Answer this question by thinking about what you want when you are a customer. Some universal customer wants include, but are not limited to, the following:

- Pay attention to the customer—do not conduct personal business while a customer is present and set aside company business if possible. If you can't set aside what you are doing right away, acknowledge the customer and let her know you'll help her soon.

- Immediately cease chatting with coworkers whenever a customer approaches.

- Avoid cell phone texting and computer chatting while at work.

- Attend to customers' needs immediately; give them your full attention.

- Be ready and able to answer basic questions about your products, services, and policies.

- Be knowledgeable, helpful, and honest about your products and services.

- Be willing to go beyond the usual to help customers.

- Handle complaints professionally.

- Be courteous, cooperative, honest, and friendly.

- Respect your customer as a person and respect his or her time.

- Summarize a problem the customer has in your own words and repeat your summary to the customer so that you are both sure you understand the problem.

- When a problem occurs, explain your position and state what you can do to resolve the problem.

- Be specific.

- Show customers that they matter to you and your company; be happy to see them.

- Follow up with customers.

Anticipate problems and complaints so you can avoid them. What could possibly go wrong in your dealings with customers? Can you do anything to minimize problems? You must convince customers that you care about them and their needs by being a problem-solver.

If a customer is angry or irritable, try to maintain a positive attitude by looking beyond the emotions to get to the root of the problem. Don't become defensive or hostile, and don't panic. By remaining calm and detached from the customer's negativity and asking for particulars, you will be able to see the big picture more clearly. Remember: A frustrated customer may not be upfront and clear because anger could skew his perception. Give your full attention to the customer's explanation and listen for clues as to how the customer would like to resolve the situation.

After determining what the problem is, acknowledge if an error has occurred on the company's part and take immediate action to minimize the damage. In positive language, state what you can and cannot do by reasonably explaining your company's position. Remember that doing nothing will add to the customer's frustration. Figure out what you can do to improve the situation if it cannot be resolved in the manner the customer prefers. Be honest and specific. Give the customer time to absorb your proposed solution and be open to counter-solutions. If nothing can be done immediately, ask how else you can satisfy the customer. Can you offer future products or services? Can someone else handle the problem? Can you make a future appointment to solve the problem? Do not manipulate the customer or the situation. No one wants to feel lied to or taken advantage of.

State and demonstrate your support and desire to meet the customer's needs. Be sure to follow your company's protocol for resolving issues. In some cases, customers may need to be referred to someone else to have their problem resolved.

Once a solution is implemented, see it through to completion. After resolving the complaint, follow up with the customer as soon as possible to build customer loyalty. Then try to find out what caused the problem and determine whether anything can be done to prevent future occurrences. Commit to constant improvement.

So what do your customers want? Answer this question by thinking about what you want when you are a customer. Some universal customer wants include, but are not limited to, the following:

- Pay attention to the customer—do not conduct personal business while a customer is present and set aside company business if possible. If you can't set aside what you are doing right away, acknowledge the customer and let her know you'll help her soon.
- Immediately cease chatting with coworkers whenever a customer approaches.
- Avoid cell phone texting and computer chatting while at work.
- Attend to customers' needs immediately; give them your full attention.
- Be ready and able to answer basic questions about your products, services, and policies.
- Be knowledgeable, helpful, and honest about your products and services.
- Be willing to go beyond the usual to help customers.
- Handle complaints professionally.
- Be courteous, cooperative, honest, and friendly.
- Respect your customer as a person and respect his or her time.
- Summarize a problem the customer has in your own words and repeat your summary to the customer so that you are both sure you understand the problem.
- When a problem occurs, explain your position and state what you can do to resolve the problem.

- Be specific.
- Show customers that they matter to you and your company; be happy to see them.
- Follow up with customers.

Some salespeople will brazenly finish obviously personal telephone conversations, cell phone text messages, or face-to-face chats while letting customers stand and wait until they are finished. That is one quick way to raise a customer's ire and leave him with a negative feeling about the company and its personnel.

Employees who work for commission often seem more eager to help customers than those who do not work on commission. Regardless of your salary arrangements, if you are working for a company, treat every person as a possible customer. Start to see profits when you see a customer. Company profits translate into a paycheck for you. Every single customer matters—a lot. Your customer wants to know, "What can you do for me?" You should ask your customer, "What can I do for you?"

When dealing with customers, consider their generational differences. For instance, Traditionalists and Baby-boomers may have different expectations, tolerances, and technical knowledge than Generations X and Y. Therefore, a Generation Y dealing with a Traditionalist's technical problem may have to adjust his or her language and approach so that the Traditionalist will understand the explanation.

Dealing with customers by telephone takes extra skill. You want to watch *how* you speak as well as listen to the speaker's tone of voice. Without nonverbal cues to guide your interpretation, a misunderstanding can occur. Likewise, you do not want the customer to pick up negative impressions from your tone, so you need to be aware of how you sound. Answer the phone promptly and professionally. Use proper grammar, correct enunciations, and an acceptable greeting for your company. Let the caller know you are ready to be of service. If you must place a customer on hold, ask his permission before doing so and return quickly. Take complete messages, repeating telephone numbers and other important information.

On a positive note, if a customer acknowledges you in some way, thank the person for the compliment. If you receive a customer-recognition award or letter, add it to your portfolio. You, too, can thank customers by sending personal notes on occasion or advising them of special sales and promotions. Also, soliciting customer feedback is a great way to learn how you and your company are performing.

 TIP   Your customers are your livelihood; treat them with care.

61: Get Along with Coworkers

When employees feel a sense of belonging, they are happier at work. To help promote positive coworker relationships, be a person who is easy to get along with—every day. Be helpful, pleasant, and approachable, not a complainer, whiner, or gossiper. Thank coworkers when they help you and congratulate them on their own achievements.

You may not like everyone you work with, but you do have to get along well enough to get the job done and keep the work environment positive and productive. When work relationships become strained, figure out a way to improve them. You may have to establish boundaries, become more patient, maintain an extra positive attitude, and do whatever else is necessary to stabilize a strained relationship. Management generally will not tolerate employee conflicts. Management will also not allow hostile relationships in the workplace because of the potential damage they can do to the bottom line. Miscommunication, unfair treatment, slander, and other troubles could have negative ramifications on productivity. In addition, the company can be held accountable for permitting a hostile work environment. People who cannot maintain a professional relationship will lose their jobs.

If you disagree with a coworker, discuss things calmly; state your objections without becoming hostile or angry. Don't blame, accuse, challenge, or give blunt replies. Arguing is futile, and nobody really wins.

If a coworker treats you rudely, tactfully discuss the matter with him. Ask why you merit such treatment. If you learn of an indiscretion on your part, apologize and see if you can correct the problem. If you are not at fault or if you cannot resolve the situation, move past it and continue to display personal professionalism. If possible, keep your distance from the person to eliminate conflict. Two people who are not able to resolve an issue may have the option of using mediation with a manager or HR to remedy the situation.

Sometimes personalities simply do not mesh for some reason, but that doesn't have to preclude successfully achieving a constructive professional relationship. Returning rudeness for rudeness is no way to improve the relationship. In all likelihood it will produce frustration and further dissatisfaction and may gain the unwanted attention of management. Instead, work on building an ongoing, successful relationship.

Generational problems can occur whenever employees of varying ages work together. For instance, Generation X employees may regard Traditionalists as outdated and out of touch. Boomers may feel Generation Y employees are not following the rules as they should and are ignoring authority. Today's workplaces are seeing a record number of multiple generations working side-by-side performing identical tasks, younger people overseeing the work of older people, among other scenarios. Take advantage of these intergenerational opportunities to learn and grow, both as a professional and as a human being. There is undoubtedly much to be learned from these relationships.

In addition to generational problems, cultural differences may need to be addressed. All employees will need to be tolerant in the workplace and respect others' customs and beliefs, as everyone is entitled to believe as he or she wishes. It is not acceptable for people to infringe on the rights of others or push their beliefs on them. With globalization, countries are tied together and their people must learn to work with one another. Racism and cultural insensitivity will quickly get you fired as they create a hostile work environment and could result in possible litigation.

Pay attention to how coworkers speak, act, and react to situations in order to gain a better perspective and learn how to interact appropriately with them. How you are perceived and how you perceive others has a bearing on the degree to which you understand and are understood. Consciously look for ways to improve understanding and cooperation, including the following items:

Tips for Getting Along with Coworkers

- Promote cohesiveness
- Respect others
- Value differences
- Collaborate
- Look for commonalities
- Be approachable
- Be pleasant
- Treat people as equals

- Be open to different points of view
- Show an interest in others
- Be a complement to others
- Build rewarding relationships
- Avoid making snap judgments
- Be sensitive to and respectful of generational and cultural differences

TIP Do your part to get along and maintain a positive work environment.

62: Get Along with Your Boss

Achieving a satisfying boss/employee relationship will make life at work much less complicated and more pleasant. Unfortunately, people can have a variety of negative personal traits that sabotage attempts at making positive connections. Furthermore, it seems bosses with difficult personalities often assert themselves at a time when employees are bombarded with other demands that strain their self-control and sanity. Numerous problems, unreasonable deadlines, multiple commitments, and negative personalities can strain the boss/employee bond. The challenge is to find a balance that will allow the relationship to work. The mix of personality types in the workplace can range from one extreme to the other—passive to aggressive.

While it is unlikely personalities will miraculously change, there are ways to improve any relationship. Some were discussed in earlier chapters; for example, practicing stress reduction, managing your time, getting organized, being tolerant, displaying empathy, and keeping a positive attitude. You will have much better results if you work on yourself, not the other person.

When a disagreement or similar issue arises, consider the boss's point of view. There may be extenuating circumstances that cause your boss to behave in a certain manner. Empathy and understanding may help increase your tolerance in these situations. In addition, you may want to confide in a trusted friend who may be able to offer suggestions for smoothing the relationship.

A positive boss/employee relationship will make life at work more satisfying.

63: Have a Kind Word for Everyone

Speak kindly to your coworkers every day. If there is something you can do to make your supervisor's and coworkers' lives easier, why not do it? Can you do something extra nice for your customers to show you are ready to go the extra mile for them?

Spread words of encouragement and appreciation. They go a long way toward making people feel valued. Tell people thanks when they deserve it, acknowledge their strengths and contributions, and tell them "job well done" when warranted. If you appreciate the people you work with and for, tell them.

Never take advantage of people; treat them fairly. Counteract negative, disrespectful behaviors that circulate in your workplace by offering kindness.

If you must offer criticism of someone's work or behavior, try to find something positive to say first and then proceed with empathy, tact, and kindness.

Speak kindly to others; act kindly toward others; think kindly of others.

64: Don't Infringe on the Rights of Others

Always respect people's personal space and professional work area. Think of how you would feel if someone went through your personal belongings, took your things, encroached on your space, bothered you while you worked, tied up your equipment, and so on.

These tips will keep you from infringing on the rights of others:

- Do not go into another person's desk drawers or files without permission.
- Do not take (or borrow without first asking) things from another person's desk or personal space.
- Do not read anything on someone else's desk, computer, cell phone, etc., without permission.
- Keep a respectable distance from people; avoid their intimate space.
- Avoid taking up other people's time with trivial things and endless talking about nothing important.
- Do not make unreasonable demands of other people's time (i.e., assign busywork, overload them).
- Be respectful when sharing a space with someone else.
- Clean shared appliances, peripherals, and other types of equipment and areas.
- Compromise about office temperatures.
- Refill the paper in printers, faxes, and copiers.
- Use your indoor voice; people need quiet to concentrate on their tasks.
- Do not take lunches or other personal things belonging to someone else from shared spaces.

Using common courtesy and being considerate of others will make the workplace more pleasant, bolster morale, and keep peace among coworkers. Keep in mind that some people get territorial about spaces like lunchroom seats and parking spots. Before purposely taking these spaces from them, ask yourself if it is worth possibly causing hard feelings or a conflict.

TIP Always respect people's personal and professional space.

65: Maintain Positive Nonverbal Communications

Believe it or not, people can say a lot even when they are not speaking. In many cases, they say plenty through gestures, mannerisms, and even silence. Oftentimes nonverbal communication conveys something all together different from what is said.

What are you saying nonverbally? Be aware of what you convey. Dress appropriately for your profession, maintain confident posture, display positive facial expressions and gestures, and maintain eye contact. Avoid slouching, clicking and jingling, and sighing.

Observe what goes on around you. Sensitize yourself to other people's nonverbal clues such as gestures, posture, and language. Read over each of these bulleted items and determine if you would react negatively or positively if you encountered them. Write a – on the line for negative or a + on the line for positive.

- Someone walking around the office talking into an earpiece   _____
- A salesclerk concentrating on cell phone texting during her shift   _____
- A coworker who is instant messaging on the computer during work hours   _____
- Two coworkers laughing while Internet surfing   _____
- A rambling voice message delivered in a monotone _____
- Someone looking at his shoes while answering your questions   _____
- Someone who raises her eyebrows while you are speaking   _____
- Someone who is scowling while talking on the telephone   _____
- A person with hunched shoulders   _____
- A poorly constructed product you purchased   _____

- A letter you receive that has a typo _____
- Someone walking toward you with a smile on his face _____
- An extended hand, poised to shake yours _____
- A neat, organized desk _____
- An energetic person at a cash register _____
- Someone dressed in a suit and tie _____
- Someone taking notes while listening to a phone conversation _____
- Someone staring off into space _____
- Someone flapping his hands _____
- A sigh _____
- A firm handshake _____
- Silence _____

Of course, without more information, it would be difficult to determine how you would react to some of the situations. For instance, someone staring into space could indicate boredom or concentration, depending on the circumstances. Other bulleted items are obviously negative or positive no matter what the circumstances.

Before you jump to any conclusions regarding a nonverbal situation or someone's nonverbal cues, keep in mind that the cues could be deceiving. Without all the facts, you may be missing the correct message. Being tuned-in to people, though, provides the opportunity to get clarification of a situation.

TIP Remember, you are always saying something, even when you do not speak.

66: Criticize Positively

No one likes to hear she did or said something wrong—that she is at fault. The fact is, though, people make mistakes that must be called to their attention. If you have to criticize someone for a mistake or problem behavior, do so in a tactful, professional manner. Begin by pointing out something positive the person did and lead in to the error. In other words, criticize constructively—in a way that the person will learn and grow personally and professionally. Keep anger, sarcasm, judgment, and sharp words out of the criticism. Avoid snap judgments. Always maintain your perspective and the other person's self-respect.

While criticizing another's work, become a resource by teaching or showing the person how to do the job correctly. Give honest feedback, delivered in a professional, kind manner. Be a source of encouragement and provide the guidance needed to get the work done efficiently and effectively by empowering the person to take future responsibility for her work. Take steps to help her succeed and allow sufficient time for the success.

If the person you are criticizing becomes defensive, be empathetic instead of getting angry. Listen to what he or she has to say, and think about how you would feel if you were the one being criticized. Knowing that criticism is difficult to hear, meet the other person's negative reaction with a calm demeanor. State the facts and provide supporting evidence for your criticism, but don't hold it over someone's head like crime lab evidence. Also, do not accept flimsy excuses if the other person is truly at fault.

Be aware that the one being criticized may have no intention of backing down from her position. If the person receiving the criticism remains defensive and defiant after you have delivered warranted criticism in a professional manner, you may have to take additional steps, such as issuing warnings or demerits, demoting, turning the situation over to a superior, or the like. You may be called upon to mentor another employee. You will want to be honest, helpful, and kind when critiquing her work.

If your work is being criticized, remain professional. Listen with an open mind and suspend judgment until you have all the facts. Remind yourself that the criticism is of the work, not necessarily you as a person. Learn as much as you can from the criticism so you will not repeat mistakes.

Deliver criticism in a tactful, honest, professional manner. Make it a learning experience.

67: Don't Distract Other People

Interruptions are big time-wasters at work, whether they are a few minutes or an hour. Having to stop and start tasks over and over slows productivity and efficiency and also impacts accuracy and the quality of work. After each interruption, it takes time to get back in the mindset to continue where a person left off.

Before you disturb a coworker, make sure that what you have to say can't be communicated in an email or saved for later discussion. If you must interrupt coworkers or others, make sure it is warranted and keep the interruption to a minimum. Plan what you want to say or present to them. Have all files, documents, and materials in hand before approaching them. If possible, set a time to meet, rather than just showing up unexpectedly.

Other distractions include the following:

- Whistling and/or singing
- Telephones ringing several times, instead of being answered promptly
- People standing around in clusters talking, laughing, complaining, and so on
- Radios and TVs turned up too loud
- Speakers turned up too high on computers
- People mumbling or talking to themselves
- Jewelry that jangles
- Banging drawers and cabinets
- People who wear revealing or otherwise inappropriate clothing
- Distracting pictures or other paraphernalia hung in cubicles or offices
- A strong cologne/perfume scent
- Burning scented candles
- Burnt food, such as popcorn
- Burping, belching, sniffling, etc.
- Clicking pens
- Gum cracking
- People eating noisily at their desks

- Buzzing or flickering lights; noisy equipment
- Offices that are too hot or too cold
- People running back and forth in front of another's desk

Some people are more easily distracted than others. One person may be able tune-out a buzzing light, whereas another cannot think with the noise. Be sensitive when you work with someone who needs complete quiet and minimal disruptions.

TIP   Do not waste other people's time or interrupt them without good cause.

68: Develop a Sense of Humor

Learn to take yourself less seriously. It is not that you want to put a humorous spin on a serious problem or situation or fall out of your chair laughing, but there are times when a laugh goes a long way to relieve a stressful situation.

Share funny anecdotes with coworkers and associates—at the appropriate times. When friends and coworkers send you funny emails, save the best in a file so you can retrieve and re-read them when you are having a not-so-great day. If a coworker is having an off day, email a quick joke as a demonstration of your support.

Keep a humorous picture of a loved one or pet on your desk or a favorite cartoon in your top desk drawer as a constant reminder of good things in your life.

TIP   Do not take yourself too seriously.

69: Give Credit Where Credit Is Due

Did a coworker help you with a project? Did someone give you a good idea for handling a situation or task? Did your boss take over in a pinch and get you out of a jam? Did someone teach you a new software program or save you the embarrassment of making a mistake? All of these things deserve a big thank you at the very least, especially if you hope to continue to receive such support. Out of politeness and courtesy, let people know when they are appreciated and doing a good job.

Besides thanking people for their contributions, be sure to acknowledge when someone else should be receiving the credit that a person is giving you. Stealing another person's thunder creates tension and animosity, not to mention it is deceitful and unfair.

 Credit others when it is due and show your appreciation for their help.

70: Communicate Well

When you give directions, do people understand you and do the job according to your instructions? When you speak, do people listen? When you compose a written document, does it get the results you intended? If someone else is giving you instructions, do you understand and do the job according to the directive?

Good communication entails all of these things and more. To be successful, you must learn to convey your ideas clearly in a manner that others will listen to and be able to follow. Express ideas and opinions clearly, but do not be a showoff or know-it-all. Avoid "one-upping" a person who is speaking to you.

Use technology to your advantage. If you need to give someone travel directions, map them on the computer. Create PowerPoint slides for a lengthy presentation. Become familiar with proper etiquette for emailing, faxing, instant messaging, texting, and other current forms of communication.

When you compose written messages, whether in letter or email form, be sure to use clear, concise language and acceptable formats. Include complete details (Who? What? Where? Why? When?), use proper grammar and punctuation, proofread carefully, and double-check your work, especially figures, dates, and names.

Good communicators are also good listeners, as communication is a two-way process.

 Sharpen your communication skills.

71: Be a Good Listener

People often hear each other, but do not *listen* to each other. Although that seems like a strange anomaly, it happens all the time. People are good at fooling speakers in private and public conversations by turning fake listening into a knack. Concentration is a skill well worth honing as it will make you a better listener. People want to know someone is listening to them and that their opinions count. Although you may encounter people who like to talk just to hear themselves, most people in the workplace are not out to waste time. They simply want someone to pay attention to their ideas and want equal time to be heard.

Listen with empathy by mentally putting yourself in the other person's situation. Ask yourself how you would react if the same thing happened to you. How would you feel?

Be open-minded and respectful. Be alert and focus your attention on the speaker; identify important information. Listen without interruption to concerns, listen for new information, and listen for hidden meanings. Avoid finishing the speaker's words in your head and daydreaming. If you are thinking about what you want to say next, then you are not listening. The person you are speaking with may drop hints that won't be uncovered unless you listen carefully. Do not be distracted by the other person's emotional state; rather, seek the message behind the tone.

 TIP Listen with an open mind, focusing on the speaker and his words.

Summary

To ensure success in life and at work, cultivate positive people skills. Treat everyone with respect and professionalism. Do your part to promote a pleasant environment while working with others. Treat customers as the precious commodity they are to your business. Treat coworkers and the boss as trusted colleagues who deserve your respect and cooperation. Keep a positive attitude and a calm presence, especially in trying situations. Remember that you communicate nonverbally as well as verbally, both when speaking and listening. Make sure you are conveying the proper message at all times.

CHAPTER 7

EXPAND YOUR
LEADERSHIP SKILLS

In everything they do, leaders demonstrate their value to their employers and those around them. They are highly visible, driven professionals who excel at taking charge of situations and making difficult decisions. These multitalented individuals seem to have an innate ability to direct and guide others.

Leaders continuously challenge themselves and members of their teams, and they take advantage of every available opportunity to learn and grow.

To become a leader, emulate good managers and supervisors. Develop excellent communication skills, learn to make sound decisions, and look for ways to increase productivity. Good leaders mentor less experienced coworkers, teaching them how to do their best. They take on extra responsibilities and always maintain professionalism.

Enhancing your leadership skills may increase your visibility with the supervisor, showing him you are a valuable asset. Consequently, he may feel the need to keep you on board during tough economic times.

72: Emulate Management

Do you aspire to a management position? If so, you must think and act like management material. How do you accomplish that? You do it by establishing behaviors that stand out positively in the minds of supervisors and the people who run the company for which you work. People who want to be in management positions must develop excellent critical thinking skills, be self-directed workers who perform duties with proficiency, behave professionally at all times, take on extra responsibilities, help others, and display integrity and ethical behavior daily.

Exceptional management-level personnel exhibit similar positive work habits and personal traits. Review the basic character traits presented in Chapter 1, keeping in mind that supervisors should possess these characteristics. They should be experts in their fields and participate in lifelong learning to keep their expertise up to date.

Observe competent professionals in high-level management positions while they perform their jobs, and ask yourself these questions:

- On what level of management are the people I am observing?
- What is their degree of efficiency while performing their duties? What is their degree of professionalism?
- Are they decisive when solving problems? Fair? Well informed?
- Do they use sound judgment?
- How do they arrive at decisions? Resolutely? Unbiased? Objectively?
- Do they handle a crisis with a cool head? Are they reasonable?
- How do they overcome obstacles?
- How do they relate to others? Fairly? Unbiased? Professionally?
- What do they seem to do differently than less successful people?
- When they speak, do their tones exude confidence?
- How do they develop and maintain the respect and cooperation of coworkers, clients, and customers?
- How do they utilize their personal space? Their time? The employees they supervise?
- Do they have a confident body posture and make eye contact?
- What specifically do they do to excel at work?
- What is the first thing you notice about them when they enter a room?
- How do they take charge of situations and people? Decisively? Fairly? Forcefully?

- How do they go about achieving the results they want?
- Do they seem to have a higher level of energy than most people?
- Are they consistently focused?
- How well do they communicate with others?
- Do they bounce back after being disappointed? If so, how?
- Do they communicate their visions for the future?
- How do they convey enthusiasm to others?
- Do they truly listen to others?
- How do they get subordinates excited about duties and projects?
- Are they persistent? Optimistic?

After observing several successful supervisors, make a list of the traits they have in common and begin to emulate them. If these traits work for others, there is a high probability they will work for you. What is it that makes these leaders successful? Take a hard look at your answers to the above questions to learn exactly what sets them apart. Why do you suppose they succeed where others fail? Again, your observations and the answers to the above questions should enable you to figure out what to do to become a successful leader yourself. Don't just mimic leaders you admire. Find out what makes them who they are. Take a long, hard look at your personal qualities and adjust your strategies to align yourself closer to the way management level people behave. With an inner drive and a determination to achieve, you can position yourself to rise to a higher level.

Be selective, however, about which management personnel you emulate. Choose people who are ethical and credible. This is especially important in today's corporate environment, where greed, dishonesty, and unethical behavior have taken a toll. You do not want to find yourself following in the wrong footsteps. Fortunately, there are plenty of honest, successful people to emulate.

Position yourself for a management opportunity by emulating successful managers.

73: Be a Mentor

Many companies have mentoring programs that pair new hires with more experienced employees. The experienced colleagues offer guidance, counsel, training, and encouragement to those who are just starting their careers. Mentors show new hires around the company, introduce them to coworkers, point out areas of pertinent interest, and clarify their confusion over policies and procedures.

If your company has such a program, volunteer to mentor a trainee or new employee. Helping others to do their best is a great way to support the boss and the company and to improve your own work habits and skills. You can learn patience, understanding, teaching methods, new skills, and more.

As a mentor, you want to be encouraging and give solid advice in an honest, constructive way. You and the person you are mentoring should decide together what is expected from the mentoring relationship. Make a list of expectations and schedule regular meeting times. One of your goals should be not to take charge of tasks and projects but to empower the person you are mentoring so that he or she will be able to perform the job efficiently. Remember that their success will reflect well on you and your mentorship. A good mentor will encourage creative, independent thinking but oversee a task to make sure the correct applications are applied.

If your company does not have a mentoring program, perhaps you can start one. You might also consider finding a mentor for yourself. If you aspire to a supervisory position, choose someone who excels in his job and can offer you excellent advice and guidance.

TIP   Share your expertise; become a mentor.

74: Make Decisions Skillfully

When faced with situations that demand making tough decisions, critical thinking skills are essential to arrive at a swift, objective resolution. Systematically collect the facts, being sure to compile complete information and to suspend judgment until you have looked at all the possibilities. Strive to correctly interpret information you have gathered and particularly anything passed along by someone else. Ask for additional details if you need to get a clearer picture. Open-mindedly analyze the facts and apply creativity and sound judgment in an effort to figure out the best way to solve the problem. Write down as many creative solutions as possible and brainstorm with others if necessary. Make a decision based on the facts or negotiate a workable solution. Document and apply the solution/decision.

Think of a time when you made a snap decision that had negative consequences. Would having taken time to analyze the problem and brainstorm solutions have helped you make a better decision?

It is often difficult to suspend judgment when you are close to the situation, but you will be able to see all sides of the issue if you can do so. Write down the information you have compiled and list plausible solutions. Spend some time mulling over possible consequences to your decisions.

After a reasonable amount of time, follow up to see if the solution worked. If it did not, repeat the decision-making process, choosing and implementing another solution.

Questions to Ask Yourself When Making Decisions

- What is the problem or what decision do I need to make?
- What is the root cause of the problem, and what are the facts related to it?
- What can be done to solve the problem or make the situation better?
- Does someone else have information to contribute toward solving the problem?
- Has someone else suggested an appropriate solution for the problem?
- What action will I take?
- How will I implement the solution/decision?
- How will I follow up to determine whether the decision was appropriate?
- How will I make corrections to my decision if it does not produce a satisfactory result?

Tips for Making Decisions

- Be sure to gather all facts in an unbiased manner.
- Be logical and rational in your approach to making a decision.
- Look for patterns where you made similar decisions to see if the same reasoning applies in this instance.
- Evaluate decisions you made in similar situations to determine whether they were successful.
- List as many solutions as possible.
- Consult with others if warranted.
- Make a decision and implement the solution.
- Remain confident once the decision is made. .
- Follow up.

TIP   Apply critical thinking, creativity, and sound judgment when you make decisions.

75: Delegate

Could you use more time to get everything finished? Would you like to gain hours or even days? A practical, easy way to free time for important projects and urgent business is to delegate some of the routine work.

When delegating, state what you want to be done, make sure the person assigned to the task understands what you want, and then *let her do the task*. Rely on her to complete the assignment, and resist the urge to micromanage. Learn to trust other people with doing the work, and don't feel threatened that you will lose some of your prestige when they get positive results. Good leaders know when to let go and allow their employees to do the work that needs to be done, and they feel good when those employees succeed.

When you give away routine tasks and general projects that other people can perform successfully, you open hours for yourself that can be devoted to your area of expertise. For example, let the sales staff put together the sales report and present it at the next meeting. Have your office staff return routine telephone calls or meet with equipment salesmen to narrow down the choice before you get involved in the final decision. Put key people in place who are competent and efficient enough to take a load off your to-do list. Do what you do best, and delegate the rest. In addition to delegating, take a look at routine tasks and see if you can permanently eliminate any that are unnecessary.

If you find delegated work is not finished to your satisfaction, restate how you want it done and give the person an opportunity to correct it. If the work continues to disappoint you, it may be time to re-train your employees or hire new ones who can measure up to your standards.

If it is not possible to delegate at work, can you delegate chores in your personal life? For instance, can someone else cook, clean, or do laundry? Freeing personal time alleviates stress and the subsequent overwhelming feeling that carries over into the workplace.

TIP Successful leaders delegate work and trust people to do it.

76: Teach Others

When you teach others how to do tasks, you add value to their employability, increase your own self-worth, and benefit the company. A strong, well-trained workforce is a critical asset to the company and every member of the team. Share your talents, and never feel threatened by how much knowledge another person might accumulate. If you are an expert in your field, teaching coworkers will be a concrete way for management to evaluate your worth to the company. You can also add "trainer" to your resume job descriptions.

Many teachable moments crop up throughout the day. Take advantage of those opportunities by passing along whatever nuggets of information you have to offer. When you come across advice that will help make someone's job easier, more accurate, or less expensive to perform, share it, but also make sure to acknowledge the other person's potential and contributions.

To facilitate learning, consider what the person you are teaching needs to learn. Does he require help developing reasoning or critical thinking abilities? If so, can you involve him in problem-solving strategies and brainstorming sessions? Does he need to learn new software programs or skills? Would learning new customer care skills help him in a particular position? What obstacles does he face in performing the job? Can you help him overcome the obstacles?

Look beyond coworkers' immediate tasks to determine what knowledge will benefit them. Identify their most pressing needs and develop a plan to target those issues. Train others in your competencies.

As a trainer or teacher, keep in mind that people have different learning styles. What works for one person will not necessarily work for another. For instance, some people learn best visually, some verbally, and still others prefer the hands-on approach. Understanding the learning style of the person you are teaching will help ensure the successful imparting of skills and knowledge. Learn how to explain clearly in his viewpoint. Go the extra step and explain the concept behind why certain tasks are done; it will aid in assimilation and retention.

Give people a solid foundation and help them build on their strengths. Focus on demonstrating your talent by collaborating with others, not competing. Be approachable and inspire others to do their best. If you must criticize, make it a positive learning situation.

TIP Take advantage of teachable moments throughout the day.

77: Look for Ways to Improve Productivity

Can you do your job faster and more efficiently? If you want to really increase your value to your company, find a way to save time or money or to increase profits. Look at how tasks are performed to determine whether there is another way to complete them. Continually examine old processes and challenge yourself to find better ways to do tasks and projects. Businesses look at productivity figures to determine the bottom line.

Be adaptable and keep abreast of new trends and fresh approaches that could benefit your performance. The usual way of doing things may not be the most efficient anymore.

What obstacles stand in the way of your improving the bottom line for the company through your productivity? What can you do to overcome these obstacles? Always be on the lookout for the means by which you can improve your personal productivity and efficiency.

TIP Challenge yourself to find better, more efficient ways to do tasks.

78: Learn to Give Professional Presentations

It has been said that public speaking tops the list of things people fear most. Many companies, though, often require higher-level employees to give presentations.

If you fear speaking in public, learn to combat the fear by taking a speech class, joining Toastmasters, or practicing with friends. Toastmasters is a group devoted to helping people become better speakers. They have locations all around the world and hundreds in the United States. Check the Internet for times and locations near you.

To keep from getting sidetracked and thereby giving a disorganized presentation, jot down specific points (not the entire speech) on index cards. You can consult the cards during the speech to recall major points. Have enough evidence to support your points, but do not write down every word and read your speech. Keep personal opinions from tainting the speech.

Media equipment and visuals will enhance your presentations, as will handouts. However, do not distribute lengthy handouts until the end of your presentation, because people may stop listening to what you have to say to read the handouts. An outline or worksheet may be a better choice.

Refrain from speaking in complex technical jargon. Get to the point. Pause periodically to let information penetrate, and save time to answer questions and solicit feedback.

79: Contribute During Meetings

Meetings are a necessary part of running a business. They provide a way to quickly disseminate information and get everyone up to speed with projects and tasks. Although some meetings may seem to be a waste of time, the majority are worthwhile.

By reviewing the agenda for an upcoming meeting, you can familiarize yourself with the intended topics in order to prepare your comments and gather essential documents ahead of time. In this way, you will be doing your part to keep the meeting on track. Encourage other attendees to stick to the agenda whenever conversations take a personal twist.

To increase the merit that meetings hold for you personally, sit where you will be visible and actively participate. Too many attendees put in the time at meetings because they are required to, but they do not take or add value.

When asked to contribute individual ideas or to brainstorm with others, participate fully. Oftentimes, employees quit contributing suggestions when they feel their previous ideas have not come to fruition. Realize it is not necessarily the suggestion, but rather the practical implementation of it that may be the reason the idea is rejected.

Without being an overbearing know-it-all, contribute regularly to meetings. Brainstorm, ask and answer questions, offer suggestions, and share knowledge when appropriate. Be prepared by bringing to the meeting documents and information pertinent to the agenda.

Give the speaker/facilitator your undivided attention. Takes notes of meeting content, and do not work on unrelated tasks when someone is presenting. Listening is an important element for meeting attendees. You may learn new ideas or discover methods or processes you can adapt to your own job. Other attendees may say something on which you can piggyback another idea to improve your proficiency.

Suggest creating a committee to handle complicated issues and large-scale projects; volunteer to chair it. Make sure the committee meets regularly and the objectives are accomplished by the proposed deadline.

If you are asked to present at a meeting, take on the challenge with enthusiasm—and then do your homework and be prepared.

TIP Be prepared to participate fully in meetings.

80: Take on Extra Responsibility Cheerfully

Hopefully, you will grow during your years at work, which will change and prepare you for challenging new tasks. Show the supervisor you are ready and able to accept extra responsibilities. Stretch yourself to increase your expertise and to grow and develop personally.

Learning new things keeps your mind active, prevents boredom, increases self-confidence and company worth, and provides you with additional responsibilities to list on your resume. All of these benefits could position you for a promotion or raise.

Successfully taking on and completing challenging responsibilities provides a wonderful sense of accomplishment. Not growing on the job may lead to a lackluster, uncaring attitude toward your work. Balancing routine tasks with challenging ones helps alleviate the monotony.

Demonstrate your commitment every day by actively searching for ways to make a contribution. Build a reputation as a go-getter, as someone who is instrumental in proposing and implementing effective procedures and methods.

Taking on more responsibility will also draw the attention of management. If this visibility is positive, your supervisor's perception of you will be positive. You will impress management by expressing your desire to invest your time and effort in the success of the company.

Another reason for cheerfully taking on extra duties is because lay-offs and downsizing has left fewer employees to do the same amount of work. As you assume challenges and demanding obligations, the company may be less likely to eliminate your position.

Challenge yourself by seeking additional responsibility.

81: Be a Leader, Not a Follower

Look for opportunities to assume a leadership role in your company, whether as a team leader, supervisor, mentor, chairperson, or the like. Do not expect leadership opportunities to be handed to you. Try to find leadership positions such as heading committees, volunteering for projects, and training coworkers. Demonstrating leadership skills will show management that you are poised to assume a supervisory role. You are letting management know that you aspire to their ranks.

Establish yourself as an employee who is self-directed and determined to press ahead even when you are busy or when you feel uncomfortable leaving your comfort zone. Be willing to take risks, but back up your ideas and decisions with facts and supporting information. Have a calculated, detailed plan, but remain flexible. Do not let the fear of being wrong sabotage your efforts to get ahead. Leaders are decision-makers and risk-takers with vision. Leaders find ways to overcome barriers in their quest to see their ideas and goals to fruition.

Commit 100 percent to every endeavor, and set an example through self-discipline, independent thinking, and total commitment. Be detail-oriented and build knowledge through lifelong learning and growing. Always keep the big picture in mind—to what position in the company do you aspire? Strategize your goals by tying them into the overall goals of the company. Do what you are required to do and then do more. Avoid the procrastination mindset by taking the initiative and seeing every job through to completion. Show that you are happy to be employed at your company by arriving early, staying late, working diligently and efficiently, treating everyone professionally, and helping and encouraging others.

Always ask:

- What can I do to assert my independence on the job?
- How can I improve my personal traits?
- How can I improve the way I perform my tasks?
- How can I become more visible to management?
- What additional responsibility can I take on successfully?
- Where can I add value to the company?
- How can I help my coworkers and supervisors?
- What is expected of leaders in the company?
- How can I assume a leadership role?
- How can I best show my commitment to my work, my supervisor and coworkers, and my company?

Do the right thing—always. Follow the company rules and guidelines, accept responsibility for your actions, acknowledge and learn from your mistakes, act and dress professionally, and take a personal interest in the company's success. Distance yourself from office negatives like petty grievances and gossip sessions.

Establish yourself as a self-directed leader.

82: Share Information

Sometimes people try to keep the methods and knowledge necessary for performing their jobs to themselves because they feel someone might come along and steal their position. This is a self-centered way of thinking that harms both the person thinking it and the company. All employees should prepare procedure manuals that fully disclose how to do every task they perform on the job in descriptive detail. Many companies are encouraging cross-training of jobs, which benefits these companies by having qualified employees who can fill in when there is a staff shortage or during extra busy periods and vacations. Having a training manual for each position speeds these transitions.

In addition, share your ideas for increasing productivity and effectiveness. Make appropriate suggestions to help others complete their tasks if you feel the tasks can be handled more efficiently.

Being easy to communicate with, supportive, and optimistic will create a win-win situation for you, the people you work with, and the company. Empower others by giving them the information and feedback they need.

By sharing information with others, you encourage them to share with you. Pooling information and expertise will add to everyone's overall expertise.

TIP   Share your ideas for increasing productivity.

83: Remain in Control of Your Emotions

The many different personality types in the office are bound to clash on occasion because these personalities have their own unique communication styles, character traits, and reactions. Sometimes, simple discussions and the expression of opinions will lead to open conflicts.

When dealing with a hostile or emotional person or situation, do not be distracted by the intense, negative emotions. Remain calm. Listen, be open to suggestions, be cooperative, and objectively look for ways to resolve the situation. Seek cooperation and maintain proper perspective. The desire to improve the relationship and situation is often enough to encourage people to find effective solutions to disputes and problems. Observe non-verbal expressions, gestures, and tones to get a more accurate picture whenever someone is speaking.

Be courteous and tolerant of other people's beliefs and cultural attitudes. You do not have to agree with them, but you have to understand that everyone has a right to his or her opinions and beliefs, and most importantly, if you can't learn to work together peacefully and effectively, someone will likely have to leave—and that person could be you.

The ability to cooperate despite obvious cultural and personal differences is essential in the workplace. Workplace stress and conflict may be inevitable, but it is important to listen to and address concerns before a negligible problem escalates into an out-of-control situation. A positive attitude is critical to constructively influencing volatile circumstances.

Control your emotions; be courteous and tolerant of others.

84: Never Embarrass Yourself or Others at Social Functions

People are often judged in social settings just as much as in the workplace. Present a professional demeanor at all times. Always assume management is looking over your shoulder and listening to your conversations. At company and public social functions, do not let your guard down and do or say something that will ultimately have an adverse affect on your career. Company luncheons and dinners can be an opportunity to showcase people skills and manners in a relaxed atmosphere. They can also be settings for career blunders and disasters. To be sure you have a positive experience, avoid controversial topics, alcohol, overeating, messy foods, and bad manners.

Some management personnel believe people are like the company they keep, so keep good company. Avoid rowdiness, drunkenness, pettiness, lying and gossiping, and cliques. Career-minded people should control their actions in public at all times.

Always be on your best behavior in public.

85: Write for a Company Newsletter or Start One

If your company has a newsletter and encourages employee submissions, submit articles on your specialized subject matter. It is a great way to refine your written communication skills, build a name and reputation as an expert, and add to your portfolio.

Research articles you submit, compile relevant facts, and write in a clear, coherent manner, making sure to identify key points. Also make sure to credit sources where appropriate and comply with copyright laws.

If your company does not have a newsletter, propose that you or someone else start one. Determine the publication's overall purpose and main goal, consider the readers, and solicit articles that will be informative and pertinent. Brainstorm the best way to disseminate company and industry news, new product highlights, and employee successes such as awards and milestones.

 Build a name for yourself by publishing articles on your expertise.

86: Get the Company Involved in Volunteerism

Many companies have public relations departments or personnel who work to increase public awareness of their companies. They organize community activities and fundraisers for worthy causes. It is beneficial to get involved with your company's public relations' causes.

Contributing to the community and helping others is a winning situation for everyone. The company promotes goodwill, charities' needs are met, and you have the personal satisfaction of improving your community and the lives of individuals.

If your company does not sponsor a volunteer activity or charity, offer to organize one with ideas like these:

- Establish walks and races for worthy cures and causes like breast cancer, juvenile diabetes, leukemia, and so on.
- Raise monetary donations for organizations such as the Red Cross, Salvation Army, American Cancer Society, etc.
- Organize clothing and food donations for food banks, homeless and women's shelters, churches, and the like.

- Solicit donations or have fundraisers and activities to benefit victims of fires and other disasters, crimes, diseases, transplants, accidents, etc.
- Restore or build parks, playgrounds, and low-income housing.
- Volunteer at hospitals, nursing homes, schools, soup kitchens and shelters, churches, etc.
- Raise environmental awareness.
- Hold fundraisers for animal shelters.

 TIP Do whatever you can to help others.

Summary

It is important to develop leadership skills if you aspire to a management position. Emulate management behavior by being self-directed, efficient, and ethical at all times.

Leaders step up and take charge when faced with challenges and willingly assume extra responsibilities. In fact, they seek out opportunities to take on more duties, chair committees, and make a positive contribution. They make decisions skillfully, setting aside personal opinions as they pour over the facts in an effort to arrive at the best possible solutions to problems.

Leaders develop excellent communication skills. They are great, empathetic listeners and interesting, knowledgeable speakers. They have an optimistic outlook and remain in control of their emotions at all times.

Good leaders are mentors and teachers who unselfishly share their expertise so that other people may better themselves. They themselves are lifelong learners.

Chapter 8

Strategies for Success

Successful people apply a number of positive strategies in their quest to achieve the most they can in all they do. Some of these strategies (time management, organization, stress reduction, lifelong learning, positive character traits, and so on) were explained in previous chapters. Some of the strategies people apply are specific to a particular field (such as learning a specialized skill or language) or involve developing or perfecting personal skills (such as problem-solving skills, gathering and analyzing data, and the like).

To succeed in your career, you must constantly improve yourself and your standing within your company. To be considered for promotion (or simply to make yourself a valued employee worth keeping in times of downsizing), you must master the tasks your company requires of employees in high-level positions. Do this by (1) establishing your goal for advancement, (2) learning what is required to reach the goal, (3) developing and implementing a plan of action, (4) persisting with an optimistic purpose and clear sense of direction, and (5) committing the time and effort required to reach your advancement potential.

Success strategies in this chapter include being clear about what you want and visualizing it to obtain it. Tips are presented for becoming and remaining a professional in all you do and say as well as in the image you project. Becoming an expert in your field and demonstrating integrity are ways to open up advancement opportunities for yourself.

87: Visualize Success

You must first have a clear picture in your mind of what a successful career looks like to you. Be specific about what you want to do and the position you want to attain. For instance, imagine sitting in your future office carrying out your duties. What does your office look like? Is there a nameplate on your desk? Visualize the title under your name. What specific tasks are you performing?

Make your visualization as clear and detailed as possible. Feel the self-confidence and excitement as you work. Take things further and see what you are wearing and how you feel accomplishing your new duties. See the faces of people who report to you. Are they happy and confident? Are you satisfied with their work and how your leadership skills influence their attitudes and affect their job?

Be Clear about Your Vision

People have vastly different ideas about what success means to them. The more specific you are in your personal definition of success, the more clearly you will be able to visualize yourself achieving a positive outcome.

Because defining your career aspirations enables you to set meaningful goals, it is necessary to pinpoint exactly what you hope to achieve. Make the connection between where you are and where you want to be by visualizing how you will look, feel, and act when you reach your goals. Do you hope to take on additional challenging responsibilities with confidence? If so, imagine how it feels to be confident. When you receive a promotion, how will you carry out your responsibilities, speak to subordinates, solve problems, and participate in management brain-storming sessions? See yourself effectively performing each of these activities.

You will enrich your visualizations by attaching significant meaning and emotion to them. Make the most of your visualizations to accomplish a task or to win a promotion in much the same way an athlete visualizes winning a competition.

- When you have to give a presentation, see yourself skillfully delivering your message over and over to perfection. Picture the attentive, receptive audience receiving your message with interest.

- If you have to train someone, imagine a flawless training session where you present every detail with clear direction. See the trainee listening to you and understanding your directives.

- Visualize positive outcomes to decisions you make, tasks you perform, plans you arrange, and ideas you submit.

Using all your senses will make the visualization more realistic and will give you a better chance of achieving the desired result. To feel the emotion in the visualization, think about a time when you experienced the same feeling you want to create in your visualization. For instance, to visualize being self-assured, remember a time when your confidence soared and try to re-create that same feeling. Imitate confident body language—stand straight, move with determination, be energetic. Use positive self-talk; see yourself communicating with other executives; imagine your head is filled with creative ideas and see yourself implementing them.

The next time something wonderful happens to you or you feel a strong positive emotion (such as confidence, high energy, and happiness), pay particular attention to the emotional feelings and physical responses the emotion creates. Then re-create that positive feeling whenever you visualize.

In all ways **see** yourself being successful.

Visualization Activity

Sit in a quiet place where you will not be disturbed. Close your eyes and let your mind get quiet for a few moments. Create this visualization: See yourself sitting at your desk working. Imagine that your boss walks up to you and commends you for doing a superior job. Make his comment to you about a specific task or project you did, not just a general pat on the back for all you do. Perhaps he says, "Your revenue generating idea about the Henderson project was terrific. I'm excited about the very real possibility of a highly profitable second quarter." Hear the sincere praise in his voice. Feel the proud satisfaction run through you as you straighten and accept his compliment with a smile.

88: Learn How to Advance within the Company

Most companies have a particular line of progression, a ladder of success so to speak, when it comes to advancement. Employees must navigate the rungs of this ladder to attain higher positions.

A company's organization chart defines the arrangement of positions that form its line of authority. Specific duties are assigned to people who hold each of these positions. The size of the company and the type of organizational structure determine the number of layers of authority. You might vie for a management position or opt to be a project manager or team leader, depending on how much responsibility you want to assume and your credentials for filling the position you desire.

Find out how many organizational levels your company has and decide which one(s) is best for you. What is the most direct path to the position you would like to have? Is consideration of candidates based on performance? On education? On job experience? On network contacts? How can you get started on your company's advancement path? Visualize yourself stepping out of your comfort zone and working toward the promotion you want.

After you have clearly defined your career ambitions, ask yourself where you might fit in at the management level. What special skills and knowledge do you have that sets you apart from your coworkers? What personal attributes do you have that sets you apart? For what position are you best suited?

Certain standards, requirements, education, and so forth must be met before a person will be considered for a promotion. Meeting these demands is your first step in becoming a serious candidate for a higher-level position. Develop your communication skills to an expert level by taking a class, joining a speakers' group, volunteering to give a presentation, etc. Learn how to overcome obstacles that get in your way by brainstorming solutions and creatively applying them. Evaluate your competencies on a regular basis and implement changes in your action plan if needed, such as laying out a schedule to achieve certifications or a degree and breaking down your list into manageable parts. Follow activities through to completion and think about how you can use your new knowledge on your current job.

Explore the options available to you by learning all you can about what it takes to move up through the ranks of your company. Can you arrange a meeting with your boss to discuss your promotional possibilities? Ask him how you can increase your value to the company, as well as let him know what you have accomplished so far. Show you are a person who gets results.

What criteria does your boss use for performance evaluations and promotions? Have him assess your skills and competencies to see how they fit with the requirements of higher-level positions. Ask for feedback on your personal traits and work habits as well.

Can you request from human resources a job description of the next level position for which you are qualified? Are there particular steps you need to take to get that promotion? How many other positions are there for which you are qualified? How often are management-level openings filled from within the company? How did the top company leaders rise to their positions? Why have they been successful? Is the path they took a feasible one for you to take?

If your company has a formal policy for performing reviews that includes specific worksheets to be completed by the reviewer, are you permitted to access the worksheet information?

In addition, investigate what is typically required of the people who hold the top positions so that you can be sure that is what you really want. What are their day-to-day responsibilities? What do they spend most of their time doing? What are the biggest problems they face? For instance, are you ready to accept the blame or negative criticism if something goes wrong? Are you willing to accept responsibility for your subordinates' actions without making excuses? Do you have the time and stamina to devote to a management position? Money and titles are not everything, especially if you don't like doing the work involved or if you dislike managing people.

Before you climb the corporate ladder, you should have a clear picture of what the job involves on a daily basis. You want to enjoy your job if you get a promotion. If you do not feel you would enjoy the required work, the promotion you are seeking may not be for you.

Working toward career advancement can consume all of your time. Make sure the personal sacrifice is worth the cost of the advancement, especially when it involves the lives of family members. You need to consider the impact that your long-term commitment to advancement will have on your personal life. You must be willing to spend long hours on the job and less time on your family and personal life.

Ask yourself the following questions to determine whether you have the mindset to pursue a management position.

1. What do you plan to accomplish at your company in the next year? Can you image having already accomplished it?

2. What do you want from a job more than anything (i.e., job satisfaction, independence, money, a title, etc.)?

3. Is your goal to perform a routine job and collect a paycheck or to climb the corporate ladder?

4. If you do not aspire to a higher-level position at your present company, how do you expect to achieve personal success in your job?

5. If you do aspire to a higher-level position in your company, what is the specific position you want?

6. What steps will you have to take to attain the position you want?

7. Do you like working hands-on with technology or do you prefer more intellectual, idea generating and less concrete pursuits?

8. Have you observed how people in the higher-level positions in your company act, dress, and speak, and can you emulate them?

9. Do you know what duties and responsibilities people have in the positions to which you aspire, and are you willing to do them?

10. Do you have the necessary background and education to rise to the position you would like to have?

11. Can you relate your past accomplishments and experiences to the requirements for a management position in your company?

12. Do you prefer using a variety of skills and doing a multitude of tasks on the job?

13. Do you crave the excitement of tackling high-level problems and can you manage the stress that goes with it?

14. Do you have a high degree of time and energy that you are willing to expend on the job?

15. Do you like using creativity and innovation to solve problems?

16. Do you like working with a diverse group of people?

17. Can you see yourself persuading, leading, and supervising others? Are you prepared for the responsibility that goes with those duties?

18. Do you like facing significant challenges and problems?

19. Can you see yourself calmly and objectively handling crisis situations?

20. Are you committed enough to follow through on every duty and decision?

21. Can you handle the responsibilities and pressures of a management position?

22. Are you decisive?

23. Can you take on more responsibility in your current position to prepare for a higher-level position?

24. Are you a self-starter?

25. Do you finish what you start in a timely manner?

26. Do you keep your skills and knowledge updated?

27. Do you have excellent communication and interpersonal skills?

28. Are you willing to accept complete responsibility for your actions?

29. Are you willing to be held accountable for your subordinates' actions?

30. Do you do your best work at all the time?

The first seven questions will require an in-depth answer according to your goals. Questions 8 through 30 should be answered with **yes** if you are serious about accepting a management position.

Talk to people who are in positions to which you aspire. What did they do to achieve promotions? Ask them to describe their background and credentials. Do you have similar credentials? Do you have the passion and commitment that they have for their positions?

Be sure to let your boss or human resource manager know you are interested in a promotion or a different position in the company with more responsibility. Even if you believe you are qualified for or are the next person in line for a position, without expressly stating your intentions, you may be passed over for the promotion. Management may feel you are content in your current position and not interested in changing. Often if a specific position is available, because of legal or union polices, HR will be required to post the opening, solicit resumes, and interview candidates. Keep your resume updated at all times so you are prepared to go through the proper promotion procedures. In addition, others in your company may be hoping to move up into the position you want. This competition can wreak havoc on coworker relationships. You may want to develop strategies for dealing with this competition such as discussing your intentions with coworkers and wishing others well in their pursuits.

Make sure you are qualified for a management position—take on additional projects, volunteer for committees, become self-directed, be professional at all times, and attend workshops or classes related to the duties required of higher positions.

Often people do not advance in a company through promotions. Their advancement may result via a title change or other recognition, newly defined tasks, a bonus, flextime, a better work environment (like a new office or a technology upgrade), or more challenging responsibilities and the freedom to work independently.

If you cannot advance the way you would like within your company (i.e., no upward positions to seek; no raises available), you may have to get into the mindset of doing your best where you are or else consider looking for other employment more suited to your ambitions.

TIP Follow the most direct path to the position you want.

89: Be a Representative for Excellence

Demonstrate integrity and live by the highest code of ethics in everything you do every day; you will be judged by the standards you set for yourself. Make it a habit to produce impeccable work.

Challenge yourself in all ways. Instead of meeting deadlines, exceed them. After completing your duties, take on more responsibility. During brainstorming sessions, contribute ideas. Prove yourself by figuring out effective ways to contribute to the company's bottom line and let management know how the company has benefited from your ideas. Be a results-oriented person who delivers quality and value and integrates creative solutions.

Your professional image and attitude is projected through your actions, speech, and appearance.

Tips for Projecting an Effective Professional Image

- Discipline yourself to be positive and enthusiastic.
- In tense situations choose positive responses by maintaining perspective and getting along well with others.
- Acknowledge mistakes and shortcomings and learn how to correct them.
- Develop a reputation for being a resourceful problem solver.
- Leverage your strengths and expertise to have maximum impact on the decisions you make.
- Be organized, efficient, flexible, and self-motivated.
- Master your tasks and fully expand your area of expertise so that you can boost your output.
- Keep up with the latest developments in your company and in your field.
- Cultivate unique talents that give you a definite edge.
- Gain visibility by taking the kind of action that will propel you into the sights of management personnel.

- Be proactive, implement time- and money-saving procedures, and take appropriate risks.

- Have a vision—a mapped plan for your career that includes key components to keep your career moving in the right direction.

- Think of change as an opportunity that leaves you open to new methods of performance.

- Grow and change to meet new challenges.

- Never let complacency set in or allow your skills to become obsolete.

- Learn as much as you can about the company for which you work so that you can identify the best ways to contribute to its success.

- Be a positive role model.

TIP Demonstrate integrity and ethics in all you do.

90: Become an Expert at Your Job

An expert is one who excels at what he or she does, someone who is a skilled authority figure—a professional in every sense. Experts are valuable assets and resources to their employers. How do you become an expert at your job? You become an expert by being someone who not only has valuable skills but also has a higher-than-average performance level. Experts do their best at all times, exceeding expectations in most cases. They are excited about and invested in their work. They do not simply want to get ahead; they want to enjoy their work. Job satisfaction is as important to them as advancement.

Experts achieve extraordinary results built on a solid foundation of knowledge that they continuously update. They have an in-depth understanding of their capabilities and talents and know where to develop new, essential competencies as they are needed. They are creative thinkers, competent decision-makers, and expend the maximum effort to tackle tasks and responsibilities. While maintaining a record of solid performance and productivity, experts increase their learning by engaging in significant projects that test their knowledge and incorporate their skills.

Experts are lifelong learners who enjoy broadening their knowledge base, integrating new ways of doing tasks, and keeping up with cutting-edge technology and research. They continually question strategies and methods that are in use, experiment with new concepts, overcome adversity, and collaborate with others. All of this takes a great deal of self-discipline. This self-discipline will help you:

- Keep emotions in check
- Devote the required time to work extra hours and learn crucial skills and knowledge
- Keep going through discouragement
- Meet challenges head on
- Avoid complacency and procrastination
- Stay organized
- Work toward goals

An expert's word carries a high degree of weight throughout her company and industry because she learns what needs to be done, and she gets it done. Being an expert is a great boost to her job security as the company will likely do everything it can to keep its experts. In addition to being on top of their game at their companies, experts keep abreast of what competitors are doing so they are not blindsided by the competition.

 TIP Excel at all you do and exceed expectations.

91: Keep a Record of Your Accomplishments

Many job seekers put together a portfolio to take on job interviews. Established employees should also assemble a portfolio of tangible examples of their on-the-job accomplishments, including significant achievements, training documents and certifications, awards and other types of recognition, outstanding performance reviews, and the like. In short, anything that shows what you have done well and are capable of doing should be included in your work portfolio.

Be sure to add documentation for attendance at seminars, conferences, and college courses; articles you have published; and any press coverage you have enjoyed. You might also include a brief description of significant projects you handled, an inventory of your competencies, a graph of figures that measure procedures that you streamlined, and outcomes that saved your company money or increased its profits. Any time you successfully complete tasks and projects that go beyond your job description, include a sample or description of them in your portfolio. However, do not take copies of company documents without permission.

Always keep an updated resume and list of references, as well as current letters of recommendation, in your portfolio.

TIP   Assemble a portfolio of on-the-job accomplishments.

92: Find a Mentor

A mentor or coach can provide invaluable counsel throughout your career. Select someone in a high-level management position whose work you respect and who is willing to be your mentor. By aligning yourself with an individual who is talented and highly regarded by management, you will have an inside track to progress through the ranks of your company. This relationship can also give you a different perspective of management-level work.

A management-level mentor is someone you can bounce ideas off, ask for specific career advice, and brainstorm ways to increase your visibility in the company. She can help you see where your position and every other one fits into the big picture, giving you an overall understanding of company operations. She can help you decide what position you would like and how to advance to it. This information could also alert you to a host of available options you didn't already consider.

A mentor can expand your area of expertise by offering her seasoned experience and knowledge; by identifying areas you need to develop; and by pointing out ways to correct problem areas with your skills, knowledge, and personal traits. She can identify opportunities, revealing possibilities that you may not have previously considered. This guidance leads to a broader understanding of your competencies and how they fit into the company's management positions.

Your mentor should be someone you can get along with, confidently accept feedback from, and trust implicitly to help you succeed.

Find a mentor in a high-level management position.

93: Write a Training Manual

Write a training manual for your position if there isn't one already available. The training manual should include a complete description of every one of your duties and the procedures for completing those duties. Be sure to finish assigned work before taking on a training manual project. Check your company's policies and get appropriate permission. If a manual exists, be sure it is accurate and current; otherwise, update it.

The training manual should be written in clear, simple-to-understand language. Reduce the explanation for each task to a step-by-step process if possible. Doing so will make it easy for someone to take over if you leave your position. If you are promoted, the manual will not only showcase your ability to communicate and compile directions, but also be a timesaver when training a replacement, which may fall to you.

Keep your training manual up to date. As your software programs and technology change and methods become outdated, make the appropriate changes. It may be a good idea to update the manual on a periodic basis.

Write a training manual and keep it updated.

94: Dress the Part

Each work environment has its own dress culture, and you should wear clothing suitable for that particular environment if you want to fit in and be promoted. Whether you like it or not, people judge you by the way you dress.

If your company has a dress code, adhere to it. If it does not, dress appropriately for the business. Dressing a step above your current position will give others the impression you are a serious, upwardly mobile professional. To enhance your professional image, observe the way people dress in upper-management positions and imitate their style. There is generally a distinction in the way management-level professionals dress as compared to their subordinates. For example, consider how the following bank employees might dress: a teller, a loan officer, a finance officer, and a bank president. Their dress would probably become more professional looking as their rank increased. Look at the chain of command in your company and come up with a similar example of how employees dress from entry-level jobs to top management.

No matter how you dress, business casual or professional, your clothing should be impeccable. You do not have to spend a fortune on your wardrobe, but you should wear clothing that fits well, looks good on you, shows you are serious about your work, and is spotless and pressed. Dress all the way to your toes, keeping shoes polished and in good repair.

Jewelry, belts, ties, and other accessories should be appropriate for your outfit and the circumstances. For example, avoid wearing clunky, noisy bracelets; ties with cartoon characters; flip-flops, and similar dress faux pas if you aspire to an upper management position.

TIP   People judge you by the way you dress; be professional.

95: Network

Networking is a means for you to exchange information, learn from and help others, and discover new opportunities. Build your network inside and outside of your company by including supervisors, coworkers, customers, members of organizations to which you belong, and personal friends. Actively cultivate these relationships. Look for opportunities to reconnect with people with whom you have not recently spoken.

Become an extrovert when it comes to networking by approaching people outside of your normal environment, such as while attending conferences and professional meetings and events. Introduce yourself and briefly talk about your profession and expertise. Exchange business cards with people who would be valuable additions to your network.

Joining a professional organization in your field shows you are serious about your career and provides you important contacts. Become an active member by attending meetings and volunteering for committees, which will increase your visibility, develop your social skills, and demonstrate your leadership abilities. In addition, your contribution can have a significant impact on the organization's goals. Keep up with the latest industry news so that you can discuss new methods and technology, company expansions and downsizing, individuals who hold top positions in companies, etc., with other members. You can learn about professional organizations in your field by researching online, asking coworkers, or contacting your local library or Chamber of Commerce.

Join one or more of the many professional and social networks on the Internet (i.e., Linked-In, Facebook, Twitter, etc.) to take advantage of the information provided by these sites and the professionals who have joined them.

Read blogs related to your field or area of expertise or start a professional blog of your own.

 Build a solid network.

Summary

Utilize positive personal and professional strategies, such as developing expert-level skills and problem-solving abilities, to help you attain career success. Create a clear visual of your ideal job. See yourself performing your duties, contributing ideas, and managing your staff. Picture yourself successfully completing your tasks and dealing with people.

Learn how to advance within your company by finding out what specifically you must do to join the management team. Define your special abilities, knowledge, and credentials so that you can explore management options. Talk to your supervisor and human resource personnel to learn as much as you can about the current available positions. Observe supervisors and emulate their traits and expertise. Find a mentor to help you develop an action plan and advise you on proper protocol. Remember the merits of job satisfaction when seeking advancement.

Challenge and discipline yourself to be a representative for excellence by producing impeccable work at all times. Maintain a positive attitude, be organized and efficient, and keep up with the latest developments in your field and with technology advances. Master your present tasks; become a talented expert with a broad knowledge base. Consider the sacrifices you will have to make in your personal life in order to commit to a major job promotion and to develop a career. Build a portfolio of on-the-job accomplishments to showcase your talents and achievements. In addition, write a training manual for completing your current duties so that someone else can be adequately trained when you are promoted. Build a solid network of supervisors, colleagues, customers, friends, and acquaintances.

Drifting through life aimlessly is not the way to achieve success. It is far better to create an actual plan for your life, complete with a list of goals and the actions you can take to achieve them. Having a plan will also enable you to respond quickly if circumstances change so that you can get back on track without wasting a lot of time and energy. A good plan should include (1) a personal mission statement that expresses what you desire most for your life; (2) personal and professional goals; (3) action steps for attaining your goals; and (4) measures that will help to keep your life in balance. It is also important to include activities in your daily life that will enhance your job performance, help you build solid personal and professional relationships, enable to you grow professionally, and make your life worthwhile.

In addition, balancing your life, both personally and professionally, will minimize stress, increase your ability to succeed, help you enjoy yourself, and help you learn to take adversity in stride.

The focus of this chapter is on setting personal goals and creating a plan to carry them out. Personal goals include taking responsibility for your emotional and physical well being.

96: Maintain Balance

Living a balanced professional and personal life is crucial to your physical and emotional well-being as well as your ability to achieve success. Spending too much attention and time focusing on your profession to the exclusion of your personal life will cause you to miss out on important, regenerative "self" time. Too much attention spent on your personal life and not enough on your professional life will lead to career stagnation or sabotage. Therefore, it is imperative to develop a routine that will fit your unique life plans, and to take corrective action whenever you feel things are getting off balance. Each individual will have to determine for himself whether his life is balanced or not. What one person might easily handle professionally, another would stress over. What one might feel is a comfortable, healthy lifestyle, another would find a waste of talent and time. Take steps to maintain a healthy physical and mental balance for yourself before things get out of control. Review previous chapters on time and stress management, organization, and attitude. Re-read the lists of tips for handling these issues that can alter the balance of your life.

When you think of balance, consider all areas of your life, including work, family and friends, health, finances, personal growth, professional growth, hobbies, and the like. Retaining balance in all areas of your life is the key to finding success, contentment, and achieving your heart's desires.

Position yourself for success by keeping things in perspective, maintaining a positive attitude, taking care of yourself physically and emotionally, and finding and doing work that is meaningful to you. When your perspective in any of these areas is distorted, your life will be, too. At that point, an adjustment is crucial.

Take responsibility for your emotional well-being.

- Feed your mind positive self-talk
- Monitor what you say
- Read motivational and inspirational books and magazines
- Meditate
- Visualize your success
- Create a list of your goals and a plan to attain them
- Be grateful
- Refuse to let problems engulf you
- Banish senseless worry and fear
- Overcome obstacles

Long, stressful work hours take a toll on job satisfaction and induce fatigue and lethargy, which leaves employees vulnerable to illness, injury, boredom, and mistakes. Keep your work and ambition in perspective so that you can still enjoy a personal life and have the balance necessary for your physical and emotional health. If you have too many work commitments, let go of some of the routine tasks that can wait and focus on the most important ones or ask for help.

If your personal life is a blur of non-stop action, readjust your priorities so that you can slow down and enjoy your activities. Build time into your day for doing something that gives you pleasure (i.e. relax, read, walk) and for spending time with family.

Keep company with people who share your ideals, passion, motivation, commitment, and desire for personal growth. Try to avoid anyone you feel is unethical or who spoils your mood and the ability to do your work with enthusiasm. If you encounter problems, seek viable solutions, enlisting the help of others if needed.

Is My Life Balanced?	Yes	No	Sometimes
I take time to relax and enjoy my family on a regular basis.	❏	❏	❏
I do my job and may work overtime as needed, but I am not a workaholic.	❏	❏	❏
I do what I can to maintain my health by eating properly, exercising, and getting enough rest.	❏	❏	❏
I take care of my finances in order to enjoy financial security.	❏	❏	❏
I find ways to grow personally through meditation, reading inspirational works, or performing other related activities.	❏	❏	❏
I do something for enjoyment on a regular basis such as work on a hobby, engage in sports, meet with friends, go to a movie, read, or perform a similar activity.	❏	❏	❏
I ease my load when I begin to feel overwhelmed.	❏	❏	❏
I keep my skills and knowledge updated.	❏	❏	❏

Ideally, you should answer **yes** to each of the questions above. If you had any other answer, consider taking appropriate action until you can answer **yes** to all of the questions.

> Balancing your personal and professional affairs will lead to a more reward-
> ing and fulfilling life.

97: Look for Ways to Improve Your Job

If you want to increase your visibility in a positive way, you have to stand out from the crowd by making yourself more valuable to your company. To move your career in the right direction, find ways to improve your job, increase productivity, cut expenses, bring more business to the company, and hone your skills to expert level. Look for better, faster, and more efficient ways to do your tasks, especially when it comes to routine duties.

Ask yourself questions like these:

- Can you eliminate any unnecessary tasks without encounter-ing negative consequences?
- Can you condense the work you do into fewer hours without sacrificing quality?
- Can you cut expenses somewhere?
- Can you seek out additional responsibility and higher-level projects?
- Can you better prepare yourself for more challenging tasks and projects?
- Can you brainstorm ideas with your supervisor or coworkers to find better work methods?

Gain an understanding of how your tasks fit into the larger scheme of things and what the purpose is behind the task so you will know where you can make adjustments in time or money. Develop a system to keep yourself organized and your knowledge up to date. Challenge yourself to consider alternate methods and concepts. Novel under-takings can generate a new zest and excitement about your job.

Write down the main duties of your job. Are you using the best strategies to complete them? If not, can you implement better strategies?

Examine the contributions you make to the company and your boss. Consider these:

- Do you make a significant difference at your company?
- Is there a way to make a more positive impact?
- Do you go above and beyond your job requirements?
- Are you flexible enough to switch from one task to another?
- Are you willing to do what needs to be done?
- Do you meet deadlines?
- Do you keep your word when you say you will do something?
- Do you get along with coworkers, customers, and your supervisor?

Avoid professional stagnation by continuing to accumulate expertise in your field. Constantly revise your work behaviors and techniques to reflect the latest methodologies and technologies. Figure out the best tools to use when solving problems, incorporating all available resources at your disposal. Experiment with different software applications and make adjustments in your job performance as needed. Be a self-directed, motivated asset to your company.

TIP   Always be on the lookout for ways to increase your productivity and contributions to your company.

98: Follow Through

To earn the trust and respect of customers, clients, coworkers, and supervisors, it is essential to follow through on everything you do. Finish all tasks, and then take the extra step by asking for feedback. If a customer makes a large purchase of products or services, send her a customer-care evaluation or call to thank her and to ask if she was satisfied with the purchase. If you complete an important project, ask your supervisor for feedback. If a coworker helped you or did something special for you, follow up with a thank-you note.

When you receive feedback, constructive criticism, or comments from customers, coworkers, or the supervisor, listen with enthusiasm and follow up by discussing the matter or implementing the necessary changes. Do not let a golden opportunity to reinforce goodwill and dedication pass unacknowledged. Always promote a customer-friendly public image and an efficient professional image. Build a positive reputation as someone who will do what she says, when she says it will be done, and how she promised to do it. Consider a job you do to be incomplete until you have followed through by checking on the progress made and any feedback received.

Make a daily to-do list, set priorities, and finish the work and projects you start. Follow through with classes and seminars you sign up for, committees you join, and other commitments. When you promise someone that you will do something, do it; and then follow up to be sure what you did was correct, complete, and had the desired outcome. If something needs to be changed, do it immediately and re-check with another follow up.

If you have a tendency to procrastinate, hold yourself accountable and find a way to overcome that negative habit. You must take responsibility: Make a commitment to get started as soon as a task is assigned or when the boss requests something. Be decisive; make up your mind to do what needs to be done. Look at your past successes to consider how you will feel when you add accomplishments to the list.

Figure out why you are procrastinating so that you can address the problem and move past the procrastination. Some common reasons for procrastinating are poor time management, disorganization, too much to do, no motivation, not knowing what to do or how to proceed, and so on.

If poor time management and disorganization are problems for you, perform a time analysis to determine where you are spending your hours and minutes and write a daily to-do list.

If you are unmotivated, work on developing a more positive attitude. Monitor your thoughts to make sure you do not become overly anxious thinking about all you have to do. Turn your thoughts toward completing tasks. Sustaining a positive attitude will increase your enthusiasm for doing your job and will also improve your output.

If you don't know what to do, ask someone who has done the task before or research possible ways of completing the task.

Unfortunately, not all tasks are easy or ones that you will enjoy. Avoid the habit of putting off unpleasant tasks. Rather, alternate performing difficult tasks with easy ones. By switching between tasks of different complexities, you will have a break to look forward to when a tough job is finished. Constantly remind yourself to get to work. Do something that moves the task forward, even if it is a small step. Take breaks as needed to recharge yourself and break up monotony.

Feelings of being overwhelmed can often lead to procrastination. Break sizeable projects into smaller chunks; tell yourself you can handle a small chunk of work quickly and efficiently. Set up a schedule and focus on just one part of the project without worrying about how big it is or how much there is to do. Do not get sidetracked by non-essential tasks that tend to fill up time but serve little purpose.

Set your own intermittent deadlines ahead of actual ones and reward yourself (perhaps with a latte or other treat) for meeting them. Keep telling yourself how good it will feel to have the task off your to-do list. When you finish that sizeable task you have been dreading, follow up with the treat you have been looking forward to.

Completing a task is often not enough; you must follow through to see whether your efforts were successful.

99: Set Personal Goals

What do you want to accomplish in your life? What is your motivation for attaining what you want? The answers to these questions will help you determine your goals. Goals spell out exactly what you hope to accomplish. They define your desires and give you the motivation and direction to go after what you want in life. Without clearly defined goals, your path to success will be uncertain.

Take some time to seriously think about what you want out of life and create goals directed toward your desires. Consider all the areas in which you want to set goals—career, education, family, financial, and so on. Set short-term goals that start from the day you create them through the first year or two, and set long-term goals that cover from five years through your entire lifetime. After you define your goals, draw up a plan to attain them, complete with the necessary steps to take. Put your plan into action and periodically evaluate your life and how the plan is working. If necessary, look for ways to improve your plan and action steps.

When you set a goal, be sure it is something that is specific to you and that you *want* to achieve it. Goals that involve someone else setting the goal for you or ones based on having someone else do something in order for you to reach the goal create an improbable situation. You will likely not put all your effort into achieving a goal someone else sets for you, and you are setting yourself up for failure if someone else is involved in the ultimate success of your goal.

Make your goal as precise as possible. For example, do not say "I'm going to advance on my job this year." Instead, say, "I am going to apply for the senior sales position that is opening in May." Instead of saying, "I'm going to take a class," say, "I will enroll in an accounting class this fall." The more specifically you define your goal, the better your brain will focus in on exactly what you want to achieve. If you expect to experience real change, you must be as specific as possible.

Your goal should have a timeframe so that you will be inclined to pursue it on a regular basis. Otherwise, it will be easy to procrastinate with the familiar saying, "Someday I am going to…." You must feel strongly that your goal is worth the time you will have to spend achieving it.

Your goal must be measurable so that you will know if you have attained it. Your measurement method will also tell you how close you are to reaching the goal. In that way, you can add more action steps to your plan if necessary or adjust the steps you are currently taking.

Your goal should be positive and realistic. Although your goal must obviously be something you can reasonably attain, make it challenging enough that you will be inspired by having something to work toward. Set the bar higher than where you are now and surpass what you have already achieved.

Writing down your goals will make them real and give you a better chance to achieve them. Some people carry their written goals around with them so that the goals are in the forefront of their minds.

Visualize your goals by focusing on the end result—achieving what you desire. Make the picture in your mind vivid.

Use the Life Plan below to make a plan for your life that includes personal and professional goals, a timeframe, and a method for achieving them. Add as many goals as you desire.

My Life Plan

My personal mission statement is _____

_____

_____

_____

I want to achieve the following goal for my personal life:

_____

_____

I will pursue my goal beginning on _____ and hope to reach the goal by _____ by doing the following:

_____

_____

_____

I want to achieve the following goal for my professional life:

_____

_____

_____

I will pursue my goal beginning on _____ and hope to reach the goal by _____ by doing the following:

_____

_____

_____

When you set personal goals that work toward increasing your job satisfaction and advancement, be sure they align with your career aspirations. If you want to advance in your present company, be sure your goals meet the needs of the company. If you hope to work for another company or to move into a different career, your goals should reflect that desire.

Set goals that align with your personal mission for your life.

100: Evaluate Goals

Goals provide an opportunity for growth by pushing you beyond your comfort zone. They provide an opportunity for change and help you become an action-oriented person. Periodically evaluate whether your goals are doing what you intended. Monitor your progress and determine whether you need to change or eliminate some of your goals or if you want to add new ones. Are you completing the steps each day that you need to take to reach your goal? Are you on target for reaching your goal within the timeframe you established?

If you have trouble achieving a goal, do not simply give up. Consider whether the goal remains viable and whether you still want to obtain it. If the goal is still something you want, evaluate the steps you took to get where you are, and those that you still need to take. Are they the correct steps to take to attain that goal? Have you completed each step? If not, why not? Should the steps be revised or eliminated and other steps inserted? Is there something more you can do to achieve the goal? Do you need additional resources to help you reach your goal? Ask yourself how you will feel when you achieve the goal? How will achieving the goal make you a better person or make your life more satisfying?

Increase your chances for success by using a reward system. You could promise yourself a reward for a completed goal or even a small treat for completing an individual step.

Sometimes you need to reconsider the goal itself. Goals should motivate and excite you. If your goal has lost its value to you, it may be time to eliminate it. But be sure that you truly want to eliminate the goal and are not just giving up because of setbacks. Ask yourself if the goal is simply unattainable. Is it an inconsequential goal that is holding you back rather than moving you forward? Is it a goal that no longer aligns with the plans you have for your life?

Times of economic downturn and layoffs are opportune times to evaluate your goals and life plan. You can change goals (focus on keeping your job rather than getting promoted), add new ones (take a class to learn the latest technology or switch to something completely different), or delete them (forget about asking for a raise at this time). Having your plan in place before trouble arises will help you determine where you want to be. When trouble hits, your plan will help you determine what to do next. Focus on the opportunity at hand, not the negatives.

Goals are not etched in stone. They should be evaluated and adjusted throughout your lifetime.

101: Be Aware of Office Politics

Anywhere people gather together, politics will come into play. This is especially true in the workplace, where people spend hours, days, months, and years together. It is the way people interact. It's what makes people act in a similar manner and what makes them act differently from one another. It involves opinions, conflicts, who gets promoted, and who gets demoted. It is about the bad as well as the good things that comprise workplace relationships. Don't get pulled into the negativity of office politics that can ruin your career such as backstabbing, gossiping, arguing, cheating, joining cliques, and so on.

Many people try to avoid "playing office politics," but it is nearly impossible to do it, because they are dealing with people. But just as there are two sides to a coin, there is a good aspect to office politics as well as the negative side. Those who turn office politics into a positive are empathetic to others, are aware of who holds the power and how to get into those positions, and are always seeking out the best growth opportunities. These people try to win over others and avoid the pettiness that can bog down productivity and successful office relationships.

Office politics encompasses nearly everything discussed in this book: being genuinely interested in others, working well in teams, volunteering for high-level projects, polishing your professional image, solving problems, company mission statements. To stay on the "good side" of office politics, be sincere, honest, reliable, helpful, and agreeable. Emulate someone you admire in the company.

Earn people's respect by avoiding the office grapevine and spreading rumors, keeping confidential information to yourself, and refraining from starting office conflicts or keeping them going. Look for peaceful, impartial resolutions that let everyone save face and win. Build bridges in your workplace relationships. Treat everyone with respect and never misuse your power or trust. Operate with the highest integrity and professionalism at all times. Align yourself with people who can help you in your career aspirations, such a trusted mentor who will have your best interests at heart. Do your work and be the one person the boss can always count on to produce the best results.

 Turn office politics to your advantage by being and doing your best at all times.

Summary

People who are successful in their careers continuously look for ways to improve their jobs and positively increase their productivity while saving their companies money. These professionals follow through on every task they perform, every promise they make, and every commitment they take on. They are optimistic problem-solvers who manage office politics and avoid negativism.

Successful people set goals that include every area of their lives. By doing so, they create a comprehensive plan for their lives that lays out their desires and includes a plan for accomplishing them. By incorporating strategies to work on both their personal and professional goals, successful people lead a balanced life that contributes to their overall well being and success.

INDEX

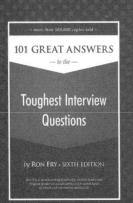
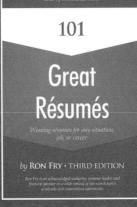